From the Factory
to the Metropolis

Antonio Negri

From the Factory to the Metropolis

Essays Volume 2

Edited by Federico Tomasello

Translated by Ed Emery

polity

Polity Press
65 Bridge Street
Cambridge CB2 1UR, UK

Polity Press
101 Station Landing
Suite 300
Medford, MA 02155, USA

ISBN-13: 978–1-5095–0345–2
ISBN-13: 978–1-5095–0346–9 (pb)

A catalogue record for this book is available from the British Library.

Typeset in 10.5 on 12pt Plantin by
Servis Filmsetting Ltd, Stockport, Cheshire
Printed and bound in Great Brtain by CPI Group (UK) Ltd, Croydon

The publisher has used its best endeavours to ensure that the URLs for external websites referred to in this book are correct and active at the time of going to press. However, the publisher has no responsibility for the websites and can make no guarantee that a site will remain live or that the content is or will remain appropriate.

Every effort has been made to trace all copyright holders, but if any have been inadvertently overlooked the publisher will be pleased to include any necessary credits in any subsequent reprint or edition.

For further information on Polity, visit our website: politybooks.com

Contents

Preface

The thesis that the position of the socialised worker [*operaio sociale*] in the metropolis parallels that of the mass worker in the factory was crucial during the transition from the first phase (1950–60) to the second phase (1970–2000) of Italian workerism [*operaismo*]; it was entirely central to that extraordinary phase of working-class struggles that inspired workerism. My writings that followed from it, from *Empire* to *Multitude* to *Commonwealth*, each time took this motif as their centrepiece in the analysis of the transformation of the capitalist mode of production, and tested and consolidated the effectiveness of the *dispositif* right at the heart of globalisation. Recently I have begun to move forward on this terrain (see in particular Chapters 12, 13 and 14 in Part II and Chapters 15, 16 and 17 in Part III). The thing to do was not – or no longer – to take and compare the two models of factory and metropolis, which had succeeded each other in economic development and in the crisis of the industrial mode of production, but rather to move forward, in a description of the difference between the postindustrial and the postmodern metropolis as a place and space, by now stable, of production and of capitalist exploitation (in postmodernity, to be sure).

All the arguments presented in this book are the outcome of an investigation into the transformations of labour that I developed in parallel with my theoretical and political activity, and they represent a testing of some of those abstract hypotheses. More recently, this analysis and these experimentations have reopened the biopolitical dimensions of the metropolis, completing – so to speak – the picture of the evolution of 'forms of the city' described in this volume. It is clear that by 'forms of the city' I mean 'forms of life'. With the emergence of the biopolitical dimension, a new analytical point of view also comes into play: that of the 'common' – that is, the effort to go beyond the interplay between 'private' and 'public', which has always constituted the concept of the city and sometimes represents its political–administrative aspect. Of course, the concept of the 'common' has always been implicit in that of the city – and yet, even when it is not denied or concealed, it is underplayed. The idea of the 'private' and the 'public' had a monopoly on descriptions and programming of the city (and on its consequent corruption, produced by real estate rent), while the 'common' was not accorded the primary role that here, in these essays, I discover and proclaim in the biopolitical. Here my aim is to do away definitively with that hypocrisy.

It follows that the contemporary metropolis can be defined as a space of antagonism between 'forms of life' produced at one end by financial capitalism (the capitalism of rent) and at the other by the cognitive proletariat. To arrive at this analytical result – which is a prerequisite for the production of a new subject in struggle – it is also necessary for a new image of exploitation to be built. In defining it, I draw inspiration from David Harvey's studies on the extraction of surplus value from the city; and I show that this finding is consistent with the work conducted by Italian workerism from the moment in the 1970s when it began to define the new forms of exploitation of the ' socialised worker'. Cognitive proletariat, exploitation through the extraction of surplus value, the common as a condition and purpose of class struggle (meaning the destruction of capitalism): this is the story of my analytical work on the metropolis.

The older texts date from the second half of the 1990s (already twenty years ago . . . how time flies. . .!). But most of the work is concentrated in the first decade of this century. Here I would like to recall to memory the late Jean Marie Vincent and to thank Maurizio Lazzarato, Judith Revel and Federico Tomasello, with whom I have written some of the essays published here – and with whom I have always discussed these themes.

Toni Negri
Paris, July 2015

Part I

Exodus from the Factory

1

The Reappropriation of Public Space

For twenty years things were going on their way – at least from the crisis of 1971–4, when, having digested the struggles of the 1960s and the defeat in Vietnam, multinational capital relaunched its project of development in terms of a postindustrial modernisation and a liberal policy. Those were the years when neoliberalism was imposed. They were grey years, although they were sometimes alleviated, as happened in France, by a number of workers' offensives (in 1986 for example) and by a succession of student explosions – first expressions of the revolt of immaterial labour – around which social protest attempted in vain to organise itself. December 1995 in France marked the first mass break with the political, economic and ideological regime of the liberal period.

Why were the struggles of December 1995 such a breakthrough? Why is it that we see them as the beginning of the end of the counter-revolution of the second half of the twentieth century?

People have begun to give answers to these questions, and these are often interesting. It is eminently obvious that the growing awareness, particularly marked in France, of the intolerable nature of the processes of globalisation and European integration and the feeling of the new presidency's betrayal of republican promises, along with the set of contradictions produced by the new organisation of social labour – mobility, flexibility, break-up of the labour market, exclusion – and by the crisis of welfare, had immediate effects on the process of formation and radicalisation of the struggle. What seems to me particularly important is the definition of the new context in which the various demands were produced: this was a 'biopolitical' context in the sense that the struggle came up against all the rules of discipline and control of all of the conditions of the reproduction of the proletariat. In short, the struggle took on a universal meaning and became a struggle 'for the general interest', to the extent of being a refusal of the diktat 'liberalism or barbarism' and of pointing to a new threshold of possibility for the activity of protest and for the expression of a desire for a new world.

However, if we want to understand the radical nature and significance of the epochal rupture that this struggle signals, we have to ask: Who is the protagonist? What is the hegemonic subject of this struggle? What is the stratum of society that has succeeded in a very short time in turning a demands-based struggle into a political struggle against globalised capitalist command? And why? What are the material *dispositifs* that determined the expansion of the struggle and of its political becoming?

It is easy to give an initial answer: this subject is called 'workers in the public services'. They were the ones who – on the railways and in urban transport, in telecommunications, in postal services, in hospitals, in schools, in energy supplies. . . – triggered the struggle; they were the ones who led it, giving a generally offensive meaning to trade union claims. But, unless we ask in what sense these sectors represent something new today within the political and productive apparatus of advanced capitalism, that answer may not be of much interest. I mean that, in the history of working-class struggles, there have been other episodes in which the ability to block the circulation of goods has been fundamental to political confrontations (in particular, strikes on the railways have always been part of the insurrectional history of labour). But today, in the organisation of advanced capital, the ability – of workers in the public transport services, and in communications, health and energy – to assail a system of production with decisive political force becomes decisive by comparison to any other capacity. Thatcher and Reagan, those muscular initiators of liberal strategy, showed that they knew this well when, in launching their restructuring so as to set an example, they targeted workers in the energy sector and in the air transport industry. But why?

An answer that is not mere platitudes is possible only if we recognise above all that, within the structure of advanced capitalism, the ensemble of transport, communications, education and energy, in other words the major public services, is no longer simply a moment in the circulation of goods or an element in the reproduction of wealth; rather it represents the global form that structures production itself. They told us a thousand times that production had become circulation, that we had to work by 'just in time' methods, and that the worker had to become a link in the social chain. The public service strikers have just shown that, when they hit the link of circulation, they also hit the whole chain of production; that, when they acted on the content, all the content had to react. And, since we are talking here not only of structures of production but also of *subjective forces* that come to be defined through them, we can see clearly why the struggle of public service workers 'represented' from the start the totality of workers and why, from the strategic place that the former occupy, their struggle immediately struck the entire production system and its new social and political dimensions.

To all those who define this fight as 'reactionary' and 'conservative', and also to those who are keen on objective analyses of the process of production, we can immediately retort that these struggles and their main actors have, on the contrary, a central and decisive role in the new mode of production: they have brought the [class] struggle to bear on the really decisive point of capitalist 'reform' and, for this reason alone, have blocked it.

* * *

But the protagonists of the fight were not only blue-collar workers and, more generally, workers in the public services. In a similar way, the million women and men who, in Paris and in all the cities of France, in order to get to work or simply to travel around, made efforts worthy of a time of war, in very difficult conditions – those people too were protagonists. The media portrayed these efforts and this daily toil with a certain lyricism – in an attempt first to organise a consumer revolt, then, once this operation had been massively rejected, to extol the civic-mindedness and conviviality of the public's behaviours while harping on the hardships caused by the strike. But have not industrial sociology, neoliberal ideology and state literature been telling us for years that in the postindustrial system consumers are themselves producers of services? How did these producers of ideology manage to contradict themselves so blatantly, by trying to set the community of users against the public service workers or by attempting to define them at all costs as two separate communities?

Users are indeed 'coproducers' of public services. They come in different categories (the gamut ranges from maximally passive consumption to minimal interactivity and from minimal passive consumption to maximal interactivity; an example of the former is users in the energy service, while operatives in telecommunications, education and health are examples of the latter). In the struggle today, this 'coproduction' has manifested a very high level of consciousness. The users have recognised interests of their own in the fight of workers with whom they coproduce the services. If services are a form of coproduction, then they are public by definition. I am not denying that there may be opposition and that contradictions may emerge between supply and demand for services; I simply want to make the point that these contradictions occur within a public dimension. So, when the service workers turned their struggle into a defence of and a statement about the public nature of their production and called for it to be recognised as such, the 'users' recognised themselves completely as 'coproducers' of this same struggle. Trekking on foot in the snow, hitch-hiking, queuing, hours of waiting, all this has to be considered moments of struggle. The power of the strike was not demonstrated solely through noisy trade-union marches, but above all through the festive parades of people in the streets every morning and every evening. It was not a 'strike by delegation' but a diffuse strike that involved the whole of social life and people's everyday routines. In the dictionary of strikes invented by the proletariat in struggle (trade-union strike, general strike, staggered strike, wildcat strike and so on) we should add this new entry: the metropolitan strike.

Let's take a closer view: when we press this idea of a 'coproduction' of underground struggle, we are indicating a concept of the 'public' that has revolutionary value. It is impossible not to recognise an act of 'reappropriation of administration' in the feeling of co-responsibility that 'users' experience towards a practice such as a strike in the service sector; a direct and subversive act. Having understood the nature of this act, our thinking cannot but retrace its assumptions: the identification of the public service, and thus of its management and its productive functions, at a very general level, as something common to all; common to all in the manner of all products of cooperation, from language to democratic administration. This is a definition of the 'public' that has nothing more to do with its 'statist' definition.

★ ★ ★

When it sets about privatising public services, the state reveals its capitalist face. On the contrary, these struggles reveal a subversive face beyond the state and its function as guardian of capital. Even when some of the actors support the idea of a 'public service in French style' [alla francese], I think that very few would consider defending this residue of the Third Republic, which is reactualised by the Fordist compromise between the popular forces of the Resistance and Gaullist technocracy and still exists in anachronistic ways, as a credible option today. Today's struggles tell us that, if a 'public service *alla francese*' is to have any future, it will have to be set up in completely new terms: as a first experiment in the reconstruction of public service within a democratic dynamic of reappropriation of administration, of democratic coproduction of the service. In fact a new problematics is opening up through these struggles: a constitutive problematics. So we have to understand what it means to talk about a new 'public nature of the services', which, by allowing their removal from privatisation and from the rules of the world market, also allows their removal from the ideological mystifications that arise from the globalising and directly capitalistic function of the activity of the national state. Awareness of this problematic is implicit in the struggles; it represents their subversive potential. In addition, if it is true that services are now the 'global form' of every form of productivity, both statist and private, and if it is true that they reveal how the role of cooperation in production and circulation as a whole is central and exemplary, then this new concept of the public will be the paradigm of any new experience of socialised production.

In short, the public, understood as a set of activities under the supervision of the state that allow the reproduction of the capitalist system and of private accumulation, has ceased to exist here. We are facing a new concept of the public, namely that of a production organised on the basis of interactivity, in which the development of wealth and the development of democracy become indistinguishable, just as the interactive widening of the social bond [*il legame sociale*] is inseparable from the reappropriation of administration by the productive subjects. Here the elimination of exploitation becomes visible; it appears no longer as a myth but as a concrete possibility.

★ ★ ★

But this new subjective dimension of the public is not something that affects only the socialised workers [*operai sociali*], in other words the workers in the social services sector. It is something that, as we have seen, has also invested the subjectivity of the coproducers of services, and therefore of all the citizens who work. The 'Tous ensemble' ['All Together'] element of the slogan used in the struggles has brought to light a new community, a productive social community that wants to be recognised. This recognition is twofold. At stake here in the first place is the dynamic of recomposition that runs through the movement, the community of struggle in which all workers [*lavoratori*] are called together by those factory workers [*operai*] who, by virtue of their position, form the substantial axis of productive cooperation. And this is the first dynamic of the process. Then, in the second place, the recognition claimed here consists in the reappropriation of the service, both by the community in struggle and by those who, in their work, use the services to produce wealth.

So the struggle functions as the prefiguration of the aim [*fine*] towards which it tends; the method – the 'being together' in order to win – is the prefiguration of the goal [*finalità*], it is 'being together' in order to build wealth outside capitalism and against it.

What is worth emphasising here is that, in the struggle we have lived through, and especially where public services were involved, the concept of community has been enriched with fundamental articulations. Especially in subversive thought, the concept of community has often been considered, as something that obfuscates the concrete articulations of exploitation, flattening them into a shape in which the association of subjects as a whole would be given in the unity of the function rather than in the contradictory articulation of the associative and productive process. In the course of the struggle that I am analysing, an extremely articulated community appears for the first time: a *Gemeinschaft* that has in it all the characteristics of multiplicity and opposes power, as a productive ensemble.

Reflection on the movement thus leads to raising the problem of the transition to a higher level in the organisation of production, where the public is regarded as a set of social functions that, thanks to the wealth of its articulations, does not require a separation between levels of production and levels of command. On the contrary, the reappropriation of command in the production function and the construction of the social bond now form a continuum. The problem of transition to an autonomous social community, to communism, lies now not only in the definition of the forms of struggle to be conducted against the state, but rather in the definition of stages and forms that will allow the reappropriation of the productive functions by the community.

'Tous ensemble' is a project of transition to communism. These struggles allow us to start once again to call the real movement of transformation of the present state of things by its name. And, while the work to be done to recompose in the imaginary the real movement and the development of history is huge, we can begin to give shape to the utopia of the movement through enunciations that translate the desire.

* * *

The slogan 'Tous ensemble' was launched and taken up by the movement, in conjunctural fashion, as an invitation to workers in private enterprises to join the struggle. We have seen how the slogan then gradually transformed itself. But it is true to say that its first meaning, the first invitation, fell on deaf ears. Why? Why was it that workers who belonged to the sector of the economy defined as 'juridically' private did not join the fight?

The explanations that have been offered for the fact that workers in the private sector did not join the fight are very realist. They range from reasons that cite the wage structure (wage earners were picked out according to the extent of their involvement and hence suffered immediate repression from bosses in the event of strike action) to reasons that cite the crisis of trade unionism in the private sector, both in industry and in services. However, while they are realist, these explanations overlook an important structural element of the private enterprise, namely that the tendency to the transformation of the production structure into a public service structure is not yet clear there. It remains hidden, on the one hand by the strong persistence of manufacturing industries and on the other by the egregious dominance of the rules of private profit, often reinterpreted in the light of financial models. The time has perhaps come to say that the productive functions related to manufacturing are on the way out; therefore working-class social strata tied to manufacturing functions are the ones most sensitive to the threat of unemployment and hence most vulnerable. It is precisely for this reason that they are less able to carry out struggles of an offensive nature. Now they are locked into a paradox: when the moment comes for them to join the struggle, they will be effectively engaged in destroying the places of production from which they receive their wages today. They are a bit like the peasants in the French Revolution, fighting to ensure not the victory of the system of production of which they are a part, but rather that of another system of production, in which they will be crushed.

But this interpretation holds not only for the workers in the private manufacturing sector. In the private sector, by contrast, service companies are now present in growing numbers. The large manufacturing companies are increasingly 'outsourcing' their directly and indirectly productive functions, reducing them to commercial services and inserting them into the context of social production. And it is in the private services sector that the rediscovery of the public, and therefore the recomposition of the new proletariat, are possible. They are possible in the private sector, in those spaces where workers take on temporal flexibility and spatial mobility as their fundamental characteristics. These are the spaces where profit is formed, as in the public sectors, most notably through the exploitation of social cooperation.

In the December struggles the invitation extended to the private sector to join the movement was characterised by delay and confusion. This invitation was made in the traditional form of an appeal to private sector manufacturing workers, whereas during the struggle it was the workers and the operators of services, even services in the private sector, who had come to recognise themselves in the new concept of public – and hence in the cooperative reappropriation of the production of wealth through the democratic construction and administration of a productive society.

Now I can return to the problem of identifying the subject of the December movement. At a superficial level, I can start by saying that we are dealing with 'public service' workers. Later they come to be seen as 'social workers', in other words as producers of social *products* and, through those, as producers of wealth. In the third instance, this identification is reinforced by the fact that the customers for those services, or citizens in general, have coproduced this struggle. Fourth, it is clear that the service sector is public in nature, which makes it the strategic location of exploitation and therefore of the new contradictions on which offensive struggles can be developed. Fifth, it is clear that workers in the private sector services, in other words the majority of workers in the private sector that has restructured itself into services, will in turn be drawn into the cycle of struggles.

But social workers are immaterial workers. They are so inasmuch as they are highly educated, because their work and their effort are essentially intellectual and because their activity is cooperative. A production made of linguistic acts and cooperative activities is now located at the heart of society and of its structures of power. The social worker is immaterial by virtue of participating in the new intellectual and collaborative nature of labour.

Now, this new nature of work is always *bios*, a whole life of needs and desires, of singularities, and of generations that succeed one another. The subjects of the December movement have shown, through the struggle and its objectives, that the whole of life, in all its complexity, is an object of struggle and a production of subjectivity – and thus a refusal of the enslavement of social cooperation to the development of capital.

In any case, as the striking workers told the government, even if you are not willing to acknowledge the freedom proper to the intellectual and collective nature of labour, you will be forced to acknowledge that it is not going to go away and to acknowledge its power [*potenza*]; without taking this reality fully into account, you will find yourselves unable to negotiate wages, social reproduction and the economical political constitution.

Telecommunications and education [*la formazione*] are the most significant class sectors from the point of view of immateriality, of the interactive public, and of *bios*: it is here that the general intellect, which Marx had predicted would become the fundamental agent of production in advanced capitalism, becomes *bios*. In education and training, labour power is permanently built and rebuilt over the course of lives and generations, in full interactivity not only between active singularities but between them and the world, the *Umwelt* [environment] that surrounds it; it is incessantly built and rebuilt through human activity. Telecommunications – which in the near future will represent the totality of circulation of productive signs, of cooperative languages – thus constitute the outer face of this constant capital that human brains have reappropriated. And it is through education and telecommunications that the processes of production of subjectivity come to confront the processes of enslavement of the productive subjectivities and the construction of surplus value–profit.

These are therefore the articulations on the basis of which the struggle concentrates on the form of appropriation – because education and training and telecommunications represent the peak and the most explicit structure of production as a public service.

★ ★ ★

The December struggles represent a formidable challenge for revolutionary theory. In those struggles the workers in the material and immaterial services are effectively hegemonic: these are the 'socialised workers' in the fullness of their productive attributes. For this reason, such struggles are located at the level of advanced capitalism or, as I prefer to call it, postmodern or postindustrial. The workers in the service sector bring to the fore the question of social productivity and highlight the contradictions that are opposed to its development. The problem of the emancipation of capitalist command and that of the liberation of the capitalist mode of production arise here in a new way, because here the class struggle presents itself in a completely new form. Manufacturing industry and its workers definitively lose the central role they had played in the initial opening and direction of the class struggle, while at the same time the workers in the service sector, especially those in the private sector services of advanced economies, are encouraged to enter the game of the revolutionary struggle.

So today theory has to confront this new reality. It has to work in a general manner on the relationship between general intellect (that is, immaterial labour and the hegemony of intellect) and *bios* (that is, the dimension in which intellectual labour *qua* reappropriated constant capital opposes a capitalist command by now become completely parasitic). But it must above all work on the bonds that unite closely social interactivity and its political forms, production and politics, productive potentiality and constituent power. Lenin had already raised the problem of the relationship between economic appropriation by the proletariat and the political forms of this appropriation. Within the relations of production he was dealing with in his own day, realism led him to think that the term 'dictatorship' could open the way to a solution. Let me say, without thereby disparaging the first person to have understood the need to combine revolution and enterprise, that our utopia of liberation is nevertheless radically different from his. We have the possibility of doing it in full knowledge, because production today is a world of interactive relations that only 'democracy' can constitute and manage. Democracy, a powerful democracy of producers, is today the substantial logic of our research activities.

Building the public against the state, thinking in terms of a democracy of producers against the parasitism of capital, liberating the forms through which the interactivity of production (as revealed by the development of the services sector) can be articulated with (renewed) forms of political democracy, elucidating the material fabric of the political coproduction of the social – these are the new tasks of politics: urgent and very much alive, as the struggles have shown us.

If we look closely, many theorists of social reproduction in the postmodern age are already addressing similar problems. All the 'communitarians' – that is, the social scientists who did not accept liberalism as the only way of thinking – especially in the leading country of capitalism, the United States, are working to shed light on the problem of the relationship between growing social cooperation and the production of democracy.

But the struggles of December go well beyond these matters, because they formulate the problem not only as a possibility but also as a necessity; because the struggles prefigure the solution by showing that the democracy of the multitude is a revolutionary fact. So here a new question arises, which is far from secondary: What does it mean to revolutionise social cooperation by democratically reclaiming administration, in order to manage the entirety of production and social reproduction?

★ ★ ★

With the struggles of December 1995 we entered into a new phase of political practice.

The first problem that arises is obviously that of reactivating the struggle after its suspension, and therefore extending and strengthening the front of the socialised worker – in public services, and especially in the private sector. Another problem will be to express, in the broadest and most powerful form possible, how the productive subjects in training and education (schools, universities etc.) and in telecommunications contributed to the new perspective of building the revolutionary movement and of organising the coproduction of these struggles with the worker citizens.

But here emerges the second fundamental problem: that of defining a form of struggle and organisation that could be consistent with the new concept of the public, as it expressed itself in the December struggles. This means a form of organisation that makes it increasingly possible to link sectoral demands to general demands for a 'biopolitical' wage, an expansion of public services, and the reappropriation of administration.

It is clear that the ability demonstrated by the workers on strike to reorganise at the territorial level, breaking with the traditional professional divisions of French trade unionism, can be taken as a paradigm of unitary recomposition of the objectives of the struggle and of the general form of its behaviour. In fact these forms of organisation prefigure new political instances (which are not simply trade unionist any longer) at the base level and at the mass level. They reveal, reconnecting in a curious way with the origins of the working-class movement, a central element in the organisation of post-Fordist production: its social diffusion. This local, territorial, interprofessional and unitary organisation seems to offer a solid basis for the generalisation of the defence of the workers' interests as regards pay and the fight for the conditions of social reproduction; and at the same time it is from this organisation and only from it that it will be possible to trigger the initiative of a 'public' reappropriation of administration and services, one that will be capable of opening a horizon of struggle for a radical democracy.

2
Midway Terrains

Notes on the productive *beehives* of our metropolis,
which sometimes look like *anthills*, or like
communities of slaves, or other times like *phalansteries*,
namely communities of people free and joyful

Companies without Factories

Hear ye, hear ye: Alcatel (a major French electronics company) and the Dutch giant Philips have announced that they will be selling all their factories and their direct production activities. They will thus become 'companies without factories'; so from now on they are referring to themselves as 'virtual enterprises'. It is obvious that behind these proclamations (and the extensive scientific literature that wraps them up in ideological frills) lies first of all a restructuring of production processes. Obviously the factories will continue to exist, Alcatel's power stations and Philips' TV sets will continue to be produced with a lot of sweat, and labour will be exploited in them, possibly even more than before – but management and shareholders will no longer be involved with the dirty stuff. Financial capital is hoping *to shift the costs and risks of managing the labour force on to subordinate segments of the production process*. And it is getting better and better at it. At the same time the production of sophistry around the so-called 'abolition' of work is growing, so that, confronted with the 'relocation' of production from the central enterprises (which are now transformed into finance companies), these companies are not ashamed to say that 'production has been taken out of the world of labour' and that 'the post-Fordist company is a completely virtual company'. However, when we consider even the most bizarre descriptions of this new stage of production, we must admit that they are not solely demented. In post-Fordist production, the company without factories does not content itself with relocating production, assigning sections of it to subordinate productive units, and 'outsourcing' both material and immaterial services. *In addition to these and similar things, it is able to benefit from the renewal of the general conditions of the reproduction of society, whereby production and living in society have become elements of the same whole; and the resulting social productivity (generalised and without factories) is captured* [captata] *by the company.* It is now as meaningless as it is pointlessly captious to ask whether the additional value that accrues to 'companies without factories' comes in fact from the relocation of factories or directly and without mediation from societal productivity. And, while it is true that the life of a number of institutions (of old-style capitalism and of socialist trade unionism, not to mention other corporations) may depend on the answer to this question, the fact remains that the answer is of little interest to the millions of workers who labour day and night in small factories and workplaces, between basements and living rooms, in large leftover factories and warehouses for the centralisation of intangible services, and in universities and private laboratories. The societal productivity of labour is formed in fact in a kind of *metropolitan beehive*, in which are counterposed or combined old sites of production and new activities that have no specific place. An extreme mobility of labour is now matched by a circulation of production space that does not lag far behind, through a meaningless urban scenario whereby now *an excedence of productivity* constitutes itself – a productivity *beyond measure*, which knots itself together productively but at the same time represents itself in a monstrous way: these are not sailors' knots, but Gordian knots that no sword can cut. . . Beehives, transversality, very high productivity.

What Do We Mean by 'Capturing Social Value'?

Moving around in these beehives you run the risk of a headache. We find ourselves needing to get our bearings in a very large-scale transformation, where 'companies without factories' and 'profit without labour' appear to have become a possibility. *But we know – not through elaborate science but simply from common sense – that there is no value without labour and no surplus value without exploitation of labour. Hence we have to ask: What do we mean by 'capturing social value'?* How do we identify that exploitation that runs through society and gives meaning to the fact of capturing value in the beehive (or rather in those parts of the postmodern productive beehive in which factories really do no longer exist)? Social value? In what sector of society, in which of its places or functions, under what conditions (once we eliminate the factory) will it succeed in capturing value? It is interesting to note that virtually the whole of the industrial economy is now asking these questions. The key issue is the valuation of the company's social capital. This social capital consists in turn of social capital proper (i.e., the productive interrelations and social relations) and of intellectual capital (i.e., the ensemble of know-how and independent knowledge, patents and research, communitarian being together and inventive mobility) that live in the enterprise – or rather live in the enterprise as a potential for gathering the value that is produced in society, both through social intelligences and through social cooperation. *The 'company without factories' is like a windmill: its blades are driven by the power of social production. . .* Thus it does not produce anything, but rather collects the production that is done elsewhere, the energy that comes from society, from outside the enterprise. The capitalists thus see exploited workers as windmills: however, value derives from the workers, not from the windmills. Now, social production, on the other hand, is a real stream of value. If we look at it as it flows into the metropolitan beehive from which I started my critical reading of the entrepreneurial capture [*captazione*] of social value, we shall see how different forms of extraction of value accumulate from the exploitation of workers; and at the same time we shall see how new forms of exploitation get established, almost *a new primitive accumulation*, in the area of computers and in the application of their qualities to the world of work. The enterprise, or rather the totality of enterprises, thus extends its command over the swarm of activities that produce value in the new digital accumulation – people who exploit themselves, thinking (rightly) that they are being creative; people who bring together workers and activities, thinking (rightly) that they are making themselves free by producing communities; people who discover new productive powers in the times they live and in attention to each moment of social communication . . . and a thousand other experiences! Businessmen like to call these things human capital and relational capital; but in fact this is a reversal of reality! Because we are dealing here with human labour and relational labour: labour, not capital. Then the enterprise grasps it, squeezes it tight in its logic, subsumes labour and exploitation, and calls them capital. Political control and juridical control become exclusive here.

They replace social reality, its conflicts, and the productive power that flows from them.

Where Is the Measure?

It is obvious that we are dealing with exploitation: there is no creation of added value that does not involve in some way extracting from workers more than what they are paid for. But, although intellectual and, more generally, immaterial and social labour is subject to this rule (and of this there is no doubt), nevertheless in these cases the old rule no longer exists that justifies capitalist exploitation or at least gives it a semblance of reasonableness: the capitalist provision of means of production, of tools for work, and of the organisation of cooperation. None of this is in place any longer (which means that capitalism's painful mystification and proud justification of exploitation are gone, too): *the exploitation of the intellectual (immaterial) social labour is, purely and simply, arbitrary. Capital does not provide and does not risk anything in this matter. It simply steals.* It organises, through company structures [*le strutture d'impresa*], both individual and collective, *dispositifs* of expropriation and outright theft, or piracy, or robbery, or – increasingly – slavery and war. . . *There is no longer any justification for exploitation.* The new proletarians are tossed from one place to the next in the beehive of production, when they are not excluded and dumped to the edge, like idiots. They know this; and they show it by building waves of resistance, one after the other, in a cyclicity of behaviours that cannot but create the event – sooner or later. But it is even more interesting to note that this irrationality and senselessness of the postmodern situation of labour, the precariousness of capitalist ownership, and that fierce fragility of exploitation are also part and parcel of the self-awareness of capital – of its functionaries, in other words of the entrepreneurs. They no longer know what they are earning or why they are earning it. *They have no criteria for measurement . . .* And it is not as if they had not tried to find them: here too we find ourselves faced with endless and insubstantial bibliographies. . . In fact all the systems of evaluating the magnitudes of intellectual (immaterial) and interrelational capital end up, alas, in the definition of strategies of communication. This means that rhetoric and sophistry have replaced the arithmetic and statistics of exploitation (and these brutish techniques of the old material capitalism and of factory entrepreneurship seem ancient and honourable virtues today). In reality, the sole condition of the new exploitation – or rather of the

exploitation of the new quality of labour in the metropolitan beehive
– is anything but economic: it is political power, it is the juridical
entitlement to property and to exploitation. Immaterial capitalists say
that managing intellectual capital is like trying to fish with your bare
hands. . . Well, they have a sense of the difficulty. But they do not
add that they, the capitalists of the immaterial, never have bare hands
– they always have them armed with ideological and monetary power,
and, when needed, with the repressive power of the state. There is
no objective measure for the value of production in today's immaterial society. *The new standard of measurement can only be a standard of
power*. Illusion and violence mingle here in tragic ways and come up
against resistance. *The measure becomes a measure of control*, a measure
of capital's ability to develop production in the absence of any objective criteria of measurement and in the presence of relations of power
in which it needs to get the upper hand. *The schools of political economy
are turning into police schools*: this is a return to the origins, when – as
Foucault reminds us – the schools of political economy were originally police schools.

Making Education, Producing Subjectivity

Let me return to the problem of the capture of social value by the
enterprise, now that we have established that the measure of this
value is random and actually depends on political power. Where,
then, is the value that the enterprise can capture? It is everywhere. In
the capitalism described by Marx, surplus value is built through the
exploitation of the workers and is organised by the social division of
labour and by the resulting hierarchy of functions and nations. The
flow of value was situated within defined spaces. Now, however,
the flow of value runs everywhere, transversely across society, but
it settles and builds deposits from which the value is once again
extracted and renewed by social and technological languages. When
production and exploitation traverse languages and spread throughout the whole of society, then extraordinary phenomena occur from
the point of view of political economy. I mean that the construction
of value (through exploitation) turns out to involve the very spirit
and intelligence of the subject. Such a statement is difficult to accept,
and yet. . . Let me go back to how we define the exploitation of social
labour and how the enterprise captures the value of social production. I said that this happens through intelligence and through the
social cooperation of intelligences: that is, through the intelligence

set to work in scientific research, in the construction of lifestyles, and in the transformation of language, in the definition of new meanings of things and their associations. . . Well, value creation arises from the work of the subjects, from their brains and passions, from their singularity, and from the circle of cooperation in which they are inserted. This means that, in order to *make production*, it is necessary to *produce subjectivity*. Capital is a capital produced by subjectivity, and the enterprise, if it wants to manage intellectual capital, either has to produce it directly or has to collect, aquire and capture it through someone else's production. *This is how education and training* [la formazione] *bursts onto the scene of political economy and, at this stage of transition to the hegemony of immaterial postmodern production, makes up its strategic centre.* It is in fact through education and training that the material goods and the deposits of intellectual labour that lie in society, built by the preceding generations, are now fluidified, offered to subjectivities, and, through these, returned to capitalist exploitation. The capitalists call on the political powers to provide them with an adequately educated workforce. They request it, they want this workforce as a free gift to them, and they concede that everyone should have the right to education, so that offering themselves to be exploited soon becomes a duty for all. But often this request cannot be granted. Or, worse, the labour power offered by the public education system has among its characteristics the fact that it is not fully functional – or, worse still, that it is reduced to exploitation. But how is this conceivable? the bosses ask. And then there is an increasing multiplication of systems of training directed by the enterprise, or of mechanisms of control of education, or a standardisation of private services. . . One needs to satisfy at least two criteria if one is to create an education adequate for the regime of the social enterprise: on the one hand, a singular training, flexible and oriented to instrumental knowledge; on the other, a willingness to accept command and an illusion of freedom in exploitation. 'New-age' education consists in this: the production of a functional and submissive subjectivity – in short, a subjectivity available to control. The *disciplining* of the masses came to an end with the end of factory: the company without factories *controls* the singularity.

Are There Still Productive 'Places'?

Clearly there are. The metropolitan hive is a collection of places and non-places, but precisely of places. *Old* factories that have preserved their social importance throughout restructuring; productive transitions from the 'old economy', which have updated themselves and maintain important niches of production, and so on. But there are also new places, such as specialised networks of services, through which interrelation and cooperation create consolidated spaces, and so on; and, finally, the *factories of knowledge* – the educational system and all the institutions of learning and training. On each of these places, and in particular on the factory of education and training, a few considerations are in order. The first is that, while we should not get nostalgic for action that is defined in space and effective precisely by virtue of that fact – such as our old interventions, during the Fordist period, in the factories and in the education system (modalities of struggle that, taken together, were particularly characteristic of the period of the 1960s and 1970s) – it is still important, whenever possible, to open struggles in defined places, in other words in the factories and in the education system. The second point is that the objective question (are there still productive places?) is not swept away by ideological misuse when you answer it the way I have done – that there is a possibility of opening struggles in given places. In fact this reply is the only *scientific* one. If the metropolitan hive is an ensemble of places and non-places, the important, indeed fundamental thing is *to grasp this* ensemble *as a relationship between old and new, between the place of the factory and the non-place of metropolitan dissipation of the proletariat.* The analysis of the precariat, as well as that of the student or of the researcher, carries us immediately into this relationship, and the conclusion is that *the metropolitan place will be wherever the free subjectivity, in struggle, will have defined it.* In a spatiality without measure (that of the company without factories), capitalist measure is implemented, as we have seen, through the unilateral determination [*determinazione*] of power. The new proletariat also has the ability unilaterally to establish the place of production of antagonistic subjectivity: this is to be found at the point where alienation and exploitation are enacted in terms of immaterial labour, its suffering and its potentiality, its misery and its love. In the places of education and training – by which I mean *continuing education*, the kind you get in schools and universities and in industrial and productive apprenticeship processes, and the kind embodied in research processes – in short, it is in the spaces of education and training that the productive determination of place and space is most obviously in evidence. (To indulge in a brief utopian point of view, there will shortly come a time when education and production will be one and the same thing, *tout court*.) On capital's side, the determination of the place of production in postmodernity is the definition of a site of command. On the side of workers, precarious proletarians and poor students, the determination of the place is wherever the potentialities [*potenze*] of freedom and production, of invention and joy can be gathered and recomposed. *Capital, working on education, seeks to determine the ordering of exploitation. The conditions and prefigurations of capitalist capture of the processes of social production are implanted, in prioritarian and privileged fashion, in the physical venues of education. The choices related to the social accumulation of labour are created in the places of education. The enterprise without factory and its will for exploitation reach their height in the fact of their dominating and prefiguring education and training.*

Beehive and Resistance

The productive places of resistance and antagonism are thus *midway terrains*, in between the old places of production and the new. And the midway territory can be understood in present, synchronous terms: it is the one that stretches between production and society, the territory that 'without' alludes to in the phrase 'enterprise without factory'. It is a 'without' that reproposes a whole series of working-class and human stories singularised to the maximum, stories of working-class and of work, struggle, layoff, poverty, despair; then stories of glory and of disasters of researchers and organisers of work, of people – including managers – of the factory, who are now defunct for capital. . . but capable of intelligence and resistance; stories of abandoned territories and betrayed generations. But a midway terrain can also be understood diachronically, historically: it is, then, a space of lifelong learning, of the continuing constraint imposed on precarious workers to subject themselves to disciplinary and technological indoctrination. Finally, a midway terrain is also one of ontological contradiction between capital's claims to control and the demand to express one's potential [*potenza*] to the maximum. . . Look for example at what is happening in the universities: on the one hand, a driving disciplinarisation that is structured, hierarchical, and increasingly brutally internalised by the students; on the other hand, the expression of an excedence of knowledge, a push to go beyond the limits of control of transmitted knowledge. . . *The hive is therefore defined by midway terrains: interludes* across which all the *contradictions* extend – temporal, structural, ontological – *from which struggles open up*; or rather *resistance*, first and foremost. Resistance, which comes from indignation; or rebellion, which arises from an excess of knowledge; or even madness, which comes from an overflow of suffering and defeat and from the production of an imaginary that is no longer able to hold in check the urge for liberation. Thus we are at a point where, through an elementary phenomenology, the entirely new ontological fabric of postmodernity defines itself: it is a productive being, put together like a hive. Taking the concave for the convex, we could also say that this being that faces us is like the universe of the miller, as described by Carlo Ginzburg: a wheel of cheese full of holes. *It is a midway terrain: this is what the revolutionary and subjective transition claims, in its own simple and operational imagery. The resistance is located in the hive, in the midway terrains between one place and the other, between a non-place and some kind of recomposition.*

The Political Body of General Intellect

Recomposition is a subjective operation; but it is not reductive or one-sided as a result. The flesh of intellectual labour, that diffusion of activities through which labour becomes commodities, services, productive relationships, and communication, contains resistance within it, as we have seen. The general intellect that Marx considered to be the ultimate testimony of capitalist development (because eventually intellectual labour power would replace material labour power) is now the basic condition of the new phase of capitalist development, as I consider it. Thus a *political body* has to be formed from the flesh of intellectual labour; from the 'midway terrains' of juxtaposition, in a multidisciplinary hive, of various arts of building and learning; and, finally, from the living flesh that is education, its consolidation in people's souls, and the infusion of inventions and imagination into it – in short, from this variation and alternation between hope and despair, work and unemployment, inventing and being poor and excluded: [a political body] in all probability multiple and crossed by a variety of drives and desires; capable of exercising force, counterpower, should the need arise; and at any rate a *dispositif* of expression rather than a mediator of needs. . . in short, *the body of a multitude, a body that includes and expresses the whole of the multitude, an excess of expression, a common overabundance of singularities and desires. A common multitude, because within it there is a play of singularities, like waves on a common sea before the coming of a storm: the storm of transformation.* It is certainly too early to start talking about this storm and about the body politic, about the singularities that will precipitate in the event. But right now one can say that, whenever this is to happen, it will bring to an end the elements of the capitalist revolution that I have described thus far. It will bring them to a conclusion by *overturning* them. To enterprises without factories it will oppose a precarious proletariat that has more productive power than all the factories put together, because it has formed associations without being forced into it by a boss. It will reply to the capitalist capture of social value by saying: I am the social value of production; I am the sum of the inventions and social recompositions of labour; I am the value captured. As for measure [*misura*], this body will deny its function: not that of measure but that of the excess [*dismisura*] of production and freedom; the general intellect needs it (and recognises itself only in it). Finally, education and the production of subjectivity represent the crucial political and anthropological passage of the multitude today. Unless we understand this, comrades, we shall have nothing to say. From the torn flesh of the new proletariat we can build a body only when we form it. Revolution is becoming today a bildungsroman or, better – as Foucault proposed – a story of the construction of the subject. But producing subjectivity means also producing places of confrontation, in other words of contradiction and struggle, and thus chains of subjective recomposition that run through and against the lines of hierarchy and control of capital. Processes, pathways: there is always a middle ground; that's where the flesh becomes body and where the multitude recognises itself as an active, creative multiplicity. Sociological analysis of the transition from modernity to postmodernity, from Fordism to post-Fordism, concludes on this middle ground. What is highlighted here is subjectivity, along with the project of expressing it and the *dispositif* of its success.

3

The Multitude and the Metropolis

A Few Notes in the Form of Hypotheses for an Inquiry into
the Precariat of Global Cities

1 'Generalising' the Strike

It has been interesting to note, on the occasion of the struggles in
Italy during the spring and summer of 2002, how the project of
'generalising' the strike – a project entertained by the movement of
the precarious [*precari*], of socialised workers, women and men alike
– was rather a washout in the broader context of the 'general strike'
of the organised labour movement. After this experience, many comrades involved in that struggle began to realise that, while the strikes
of factory workers 'hurt' the boss, the social strike slipped, so to
speak, through the folds of the global working day: it did no harm to
the bosses but did not bring any benefit to the flexible mobile workers
either. This finding raises a problem: that of understanding how the
socialised workers choose to struggle and how, within the space of
the metropolis, they can overturn subordination in production and
the violence of exploitation. In other words, we need to ask in what
relation the metropolis stands to the multitude and whether it is
correct to say that the metropolis is to the multitude what the factory
was to the working class. This hypothesis appears as something of a
problem – one raised not just by the obvious differences in immediate
effectiveness between social struggles and factory struggles, but also
by a more relevant general question. If the metropolis has become
invested with capitalist relations of value production and exploitation, then how can one grasp the antagonism of the metropolitan
multitude within the metropolis? In the 1960s and 1970s, as these
problems arose in relation to the struggles of the working class and
changes in metropolitan lifestyles, various answers were given; and

often they were very effective. I summarise them in what follows. For the moment, it is worth pointing out how those answers referred to an external relationship between the working class and other metropolitan layers of wage labour and intellectual labour. Today the problem is posed differently, because the various sections of labour power present themselves in the hybridity of the metropolis as an internal relationship, namely immediately as multitude: as an overall reality made up of singularities, a multiplicity of groups and subjectivities, which (antagonistically) shape the space of the metropolis.

2 Theoretical Anticipations

Among the scholars of the metropolis (architects and urbanists), it was Rem Koolhaas who gave us, in the late 1970s, in delirious terms, a first new image of the metropolis. I am talking, of course, about *Delirious New York*. What was the central thesis of this book? It consisted in giving us an image of the metropolis – which, both beyond and through plannings (these were always more or less coherently developed on it), nevertheless lived dynamics, conflicts and powerful overlappings of cultural strata, of forms and styles of life, of a multiplicity of hypotheses and projects for the future. To understand the city, you had to view this complexity, this microphysics of potentialities, from within. New York, in particular, was an example of an extraordinary historical, political, technological and artistic accumulation of various forms of urban programming. But this was not enough. Additionally it had to be said that the metropolis was stronger than the urban. Speculative interests and the resistance of the citizens at once defeated and overwhelmed both the prescriptions of power and the utopias of its opponents. The fact is that the metropolis jumbled and mixed the terms of urbanistic discourse: starting from a given urban intensity, the metropolis was creating new categories, it was a new proliferating machine. Measure extended beyond measure. So the question was to provide at once a microphysical analysis of the metropolis – of New York in this case – that could account both for the thousands and thousands of acting singularities and for the forms of repression and blockade that the power [*potenza*] of the multitude encountered. This is how Koolhaas' architecture rises through large-scale measures of urban coexistence, which are then overturned, changed and mixed with other architectural forms. . . What Koolhaas' architecture expresses is a grand narrative, the grand narrative of the destruction of the western city, which then gives way to a mixed-race metropolis. It is not relevant (although it is helpful to understand) that in Koolhaas architectural development is classified depending on the various techniques of building construction work. What interests me is exactly the opposite: albeit through an industrial corporativisation of the agents of production, here we perceive how at this stage the metropolis organises itself at levels that are continuous but distorted, faithful to the welfare state but hybrid. The metropolis is a common world. It is the product of all – not a general will but a shared randomness.

So the metropolis seeks to be imperial. The weak postmodernists are beaten in the breach by Koolhaas. In fact, probing the genealogy of the metropolis, Koolhaas anticipates an operation that becomes crucial in mature postmodernism: the recognition of the global dimension as being more productive and more generous in types of economies and lifestyles. This critical effort is not solitary or neutralising. On the contrary, it produces further critique and entrusts it to the real movement. For example, when we introduce elements of difference and antagonism into the knowledge of the city and turn them into the engine of metropolitan construction, we also compose new frameworks of living and of struggling – common ones. Another example, among others, would be metropolis and collectivisation. This old socialist word is by now obsolete and completely left behind in the minds of the younger generation. But that's not the problem. The project is not to collectivise but to recognise and organise the common. A common made of a very rich heritage of lifestyles, of collective means of communication and reproduction of life – and, especially, of excedence in the common expression of life in metropolitan areas. We are enjoying a second generation of metropolitan life, which is creative of cooperation and is excedent in the immaterial, relational and linguistic values that it produces. So there we have it, the metropolis of the singular and collective multitude.

There are many postmodernists who reject the possibility of regarding the metropolis of the multitude as a collective and singular space, massively common, subjectively malleable, and always invented anew. Such refusals put the analyst in the position of the jester or the sycophant of power. We, for our part, have recovered the ideas of economic externalities, of immaterial dynamics, of cycles of struggle and everything that makes up the multitude. New York is postmodern insofar as it has participated in all degrees of the modern and has, so to speak, consumed them in critique and in the prefiguration of the alternative. The result is a hybrid: the metropolitan hybrid as a spatial and temporal symbol of struggles – a project of the microphysics of powers.

3 Metropolis and Global Space

Saskia Sassen was the first to teach us to see the metropolis, all metropolises, not only as in Koolhaas, as a hybrid and self-conflicting aggregate, but as a homologous image of the general structure that capitalism has assumed in the imperial phase; and she has done so more than anyone else. Metropolises express and individualise the consolidation of the global hierarchy at its most articulated points, in a complex of forms and exercise of command. Class differences and generic programming in the division of labour are now not done between nations but between centre and periphery, in metropolises. Sassen goes to look at skyscrapers and draws from them harsh lessons. At the top are those who command; below, those who obey. In the isolated space of those who are higher up resides the connection with the world, while in the communications of those who are lower down reside the mobile points, the lifestyles and renewed functions of metropolitan recomposition. For this reason, we have to traverse the possible spaces of the metropolis if we want to retie the threads of the struggle, to discover the channels and forms of connection, the ways in which the subjects fit together. Sassen suggests that we view skyscrapers as a structure of imperial unification. But at the same time she offers the subtle and provocative proposal of imagining the skyscraper not as a whole, but as an above and a below. Between the above and the below runs the relation of command, of exploitation, and hence the possibility of revolt.

Sassen's proposals had a powerful impact in Europe in the 1990s, when, with some difficulty but nonetheless effectively, some antagonistic forces started seeing the structure of the city as a reflection of the contradictions of globalisation. In fact, whether there are skyscrapers or not, the global order reestablished in the metropolis an above and below that belonged to a relation of exploitation that stretched across the internal horizon of urban society. Sassen showed the places and relations of exploitation and dissolved the multitude, bringing it back to the dispersed exercise of material activities. On the other hand, there is command. Blade Runner becomes scientific reality.

4 Historical Anticipations

But others see the metropolises of skyscrapers and of Empire rather as places of struggle that can reveal aspects of the common and, above all, can embody pathways and organisations of resistance and subversion. Here the example that immediately comes to mind is that of the Parisian struggles of winter 1995–6. Those struggles were memorable because on that occasion the plans for privatising public transport in Paris were rejected not only by the unions but by the combined struggles of much of the metropolitan population. However, those struggles would never have assumed the intensity and importance they had, had they not been traversed and, somehow, already prefigured by the struggles of the *sans-papiers*, the homeless, the unemployed and so on. In other words, the vast complexity of the metropolis opens escape routes for all the urban poor: this is where the metropolis, even an imperial one, wakes up to antagonism.

These developments and these antagonisms were already evident in the 1970s: in Germany, in the United States, and in Italy. The big transition from the battlefield of the factory to that of the metropolis, from class to multitude, was lived and organised, theoretically and practically, by very many vanguards. 'Let's take over the city' [*Prendiamoci la città*] was one of the key slogans in Italy – persistent, important and overwhelming. Similar slogans were found in the German Bürger-Initiativen, and also in the experiences of squatters in nearly all European cities. Factory workers recognised themselves in this development but the leaders of trade unions and of the parties of the labour movement ignored it. The 'no-ticket' strikes on transport systems, the massive occupations of housing, the organisation of working-class leisure activities in local neighbourhoods and of workers' security against police and tax collectors, and so on – in short, the seizure of zones of the city was a project very carefully pursued. Such areas were called 'red bases' in those days. Often, though, they were not places but urban spaces, places of public opinion. Sometimes they also happened to be decidedly non-places – or rather they were mass demonstrations in motion, travelling along and occupying squares and territories. Thus the metropolis began to be rebuilt by a strange alliance: factory workers and metropolitan proletarians. Here we began to see how powerful this alliance was.

At the base of these political experiences was also another, broader theoretical experiment. From the early 1970s on people began to realise that the metropolis was not only invaded by globalisation from the top of skyscrapers but also created by the transformations in labour that were coming about. In the 1970s Alberto Magnaghi and his comrades published a remarkable journal, *Quaderni del territorio*, which showed, in each issue more convincingly, how capital was investing the city, turning every street into a productive flow of goods. The factory had thus extended into and onto society: this was obvious. But it was also clear that this productive investment of the city radically modified the class confrontation.

5   Police and War

In the 1990s the great transformation of the relations of production, which invest the metropolis, reaches its quantitative limit and configures a new phase. The capitalist recomposition of the city – or rather of the metropolis – is given in all the complexity of the new configuration of power relations in the Empire. It was Mike Davis who first offered an appropriate representation of the phenomena characteristic of the postmodern metropolis: the erection of walls intended to delimit areas closed to the poor; the definition of ghettos or slum areas where the desperate of the earth could accumulate; the disciplining of the lines of flow and control that maintained order; a preventive analysis and practice of containing and monitoring eventual interruptions of the cycle. When people talk today, in imperial literature, of continuity between global war and policing, they forget to say this one thing, that the continuous and homogeneous techniques of war and policing were invented in the metropolis. 'Zero tolerance' has become a buzzword, or rather a preventive device that invests entire social strata while targeting single individuals, intractable or excluded. Every now and then racial colour or religious dress, particular ways of life or class difference are taken as the defining parameters of repressive zoning in the metropolis. The metropolis is constructed on these mechanisms. As I said about the work of Sassen, the spatial dimensions, the width and height of buildings and public spaces are completely subordinated to the logic of control. This happens where it is possible; but where real estate imposes rents that are too high to be used as instruments of direct control, through the application of heavy urban programming, the metropolitan landscape is covered in networks of electronic control, traversed and marked by representations of danger in the shape of closed-circuit television and helicopters. Soon all cities will be crowded with the kind of automated instruments of control – unmanned aircraft, police drones – that armies normally use in wars. Soon the enclosures and the red zones will follow the logic of overflights: urban planning will then have to internalise forms of control based on an aerial globality, as precondition of the freedom to develop spaces and society. Obviously, in saying this I am overstating a number of trends that are still limited in scope and represent only part of the development of the metropolis. Indeed, here too (as in the theory of war), the enormous ability to develop violence on the side of power, the so-called total asymmetry, generates matching responses: the phantasm of David versus the reality of Goliath. Hence the planification of control over the city and the 'zero tolerance' produce new forms of resistance in the same way. The metropolitan network is continuously interrupted – sometimes disrupted – by networks of resistance. The capitalist recomposition of the metropolis builds traces of recomposition for the multitude. The fact is that, in order to exist, control itself has to recognise, or even construct, transindividual patterns of citizenship. All urban sociology, from the Chicago School to the present day, knows that even within a framework of extreme individualism the concepts and the schemes of interpretation must assume dimensions that are transindividual, almost communitarian. It is to the development of these forms of life that analysis has to apply itself. This will lead to the discovery, in the metropolis, of defined spaces, of precise localisations of the multitude. Spatial and temporal determinations of habitat and of the wage (consumption) will be found to mark out the contours of districts and to characterise the behaviour of populations. War as a legitimation of order, the police as an instrument of order – these powers that have taken a constituent function in the metropolis, replacing citizens and movements: well, they will not get through. Once again, the analysis of the metropolis leads here to the perception of the excedence of value that is produced through the cooperation of immaterial labour. The crisis of the metropolis has thus taken a big step forward.

6 Building the Metropolitan Strike

I was told that in Seville, when the 'generalised strike' – it was a 24-hour strike – was launched during the night in all neighbourhoods, people formed flying pickets and from midnight onwards blocked transportation, closed the night clubs, and communicated to the city the urgency of the struggle. And this continued with a general mobilisation across the metropolis that, in the afternoon, aggregated in mass demonstrations that continued throughout the day. This is a good example of the management of a generalised strike. It is a metropolitan strike in which the various sectors of social labour come together throughout the 24 hours of the working day. But all this, this formidable political movement, seems insufficient for an adequate definition of the 'generalised strike'. We need a deeper approach, a specific analysis of each phase and movement of recomposition, of every moment of struggle that can flow together into the construction of the social strike. Why do I say this? Because I see the metropolitan strike as the specific form of recomposition of the multitude in the metropolis. The metropolitan strike is not a socialisation of the factory workers' strike; it is a new form of counterpower. How it will act in time and space we do not yet know. What we do know is that a functionalist sociology – of the kind that brings together the various segments of the social recomposition of labour under capitalist control – will not be sufficient to define the metropolitan strike. The encounter, the clash, the engagement and forward motion of the various strata of the metropolitan multitude can be indicated only as the construction (in struggle) of movements of power [*potenza*]. But on what basis does the movement become a deployed capacity for power [*potenza*]? For me, the answer certainly does not entail storming the Winter Palace. Metropolitan revolts do not ask for the mayor to be replaced; they express new forms of democracy, forms that are the opposite of those involved in the control of the metropolis. Metropolitan revolt is always a refounding of the city.

7 Rebuilding the Metropolis

The 'generalised strike' must therefore contain in itself the 'delirious' project of rebuilding the metropolis. What does this mean, to rebuild the metropolis? It means refinding the common and constructing metropolitan proximities. We have two figures that are absolutely indicative of this project and place themselves at the extreme ends of a scale of commonness: the firefighter and the immigrant. The firefighter represents the common as security, as everyone's recourse in the event of danger, as a constructor in the common imagination of children; the immigrant is the person needed to give colour to the metropolis as well as meaning to solidarity. The firefighter is the danger, the immigrant is hope. The firefighter is insecurity, the immigrant is the future. When we think of the metropolis, we think of it as a physical commonness that consists of wealth and production of cultural community. Nothing indicates better than the metropolis the design of a sustainable development, a synthesis of ecology and production, in short, a biopolitical framework. Today, precisely in this period, we are bearing the brunt of a series of old patterns of social democracy, which are no less ignoble for being powerless. They tell us that the metropolis can reproduce itself only if social safety nets are introduced that serve to monetise (and possibly repair) the dramatic effects of capitalist development. Politicians and corrupt unions are negotiating the detail of those safety nets. . . In my view, however, the metropolis is a resource, an exceptional and excessive resource, even when the city is made up of favelas, shacks, and chaos. You cannot impose on the city schemes of order anticipated through omnipotent control (at ground level and from the sky, through war and policing) or structures of neutralisation (repression, safety nets, and so on) that seek to operate within the social fabric. The metropolis is free. The freedom of the metropolis is born from the construction and reconstruction that it operates itself on itself, every day. The 'generalised strike' is part of this framework. It is an extension, or rather manifestation or revelation, of what lives in the depths of the city. Probably in Seville the 'generalised strike' was also this thing: the discovery of that other society that lives in the metropolis during the entire time of the working day. We do not know whether this is how things really went. However, what I want to emphasise is that the 'generalised strike' is a kind of radical excavation of the life of the metropolis, of its production structure, of its common.

4

Exiting from Industrial Capitalism

Review of Carlo Vercellone, ed., Reddito di cittadinanza come dispositivo costituente 'intermezzo' [Citizen Income as an 'Intermediary' Constituent Mechanism]

This book renews a traditional analysis of the transformations in capitalism, which takes as its starting point the hypothesis of the structuring role of changes in the division of labour: starting from the reality of these transformations, it asks whether we are perhaps in a twilight of industrial capitalism. The authors who have accepted the challenge of this question are about twenty in number. To give an idea of the development of the ideas in the book, I shall have to limit myself to a few specific headings that seem to work particularly well in the debate, regrettably neglecting others.

The contributions gathered in the book are organised around the following questions: is it possible that the current development of the organisation of work and of the knowledge economy signals the end of the logic according to which, from Adam Smith onwards, the technical and organisational division of labour was seen as the determing factor in productivity? Second, if we answer this in the affirmative, in what sense do the diffusion and driving role of knowledge define the opening of a post-Smithian twenty-first century? And, finally, in what ways do the various models that describe the knowledge economy take account of the current transformations in the division of labour and of the new dualisms in the domestic and global labour markets? To these questions others can be added: What is the role of money in the transition to cognitive capitalism? What are the forms of articulation and capture of cognitive values by finance capital? Also, what are the possible scenarios of an evolution in the regulation of the wage relation? Is the American neoliberal model the only possible one, or are there alternatives to it? As for the transformation of the productive and financial spheres, does it open the way to new rules of wealth distribution? In particular, does the question of a guaranteed income, independent of employment, find new theoretical foundations when we take into account the increasingly social nature of the growth in productivity and the positive externalities that derive from the spread, the driving *dispositif* and the excedence of knowledge?

In order to address these questions, the book edited by Carlo Vercellone sets itself the task of combining the new theoretical contributions with a historical overview of capitalist economy, thereby creating an account that addresses the long-term dynamics of development. When you assume a structuring role for changes in the division of labour, you are more or less obliged to undertake an in-depth historical study. The polemic regarding continuity and discontinuity in economic development (particularly around the current transition from modernity to postmodernity) is very much in the air. The same applies to research in two fields contiguous with political economy, namely sociology and political science: at stake here, through the analysis of the evolution of the division of labour, is a clarification of the transformations of labour – in other words, if we go a little deeper, the transformation of ontology and the radical mutation in the anthropology of work.

> First: we have a number of contributions to the definition of a new era in the division of labour (both domestic and international).

Remy Herrera and Carlo Vercellone, in their article 'Transformations in the Division of Labour and General Intellect', highlight the topicality of Marx's hypothesis of the general intellect in the long-term dynamic of capitalism.

With this concept Marx opened the possibility of a new post-industrial phase in the division of labour, one in which knowledge, as it gets socialised, becomes the primary force of production. This would result in a crisis of the logic of real subsumption proper to the hegemony of industrial capitalism, and in a consequent shift in the traditional terms of opposition between capital and labour – namely in the direction of a new antagonism between the *living knowledge* of labour and the *dead knowledge* of capital. The authors show the impotence of the theoretical innovations of neoclassical economics when it finds itself having to deal with the new realities of cognitive capitalism. They also show the extent to which the capitalist world of real subsumption is traversed, hollowed out [*scavato*] and thrown into contradiction by the struggles, or simply by the behaviours, of the new cognitive labour power.

Pierre Dockès, in his article 'Metacapitalism and Transformations in the System of Production', moves on the same terrain: on the one hand, the crisis of the Fordist model of regulating the wage relation and of its management by the state is the outcome of a complex historical dialectic of conflicts and innovations; on the other, it leads to a deep refoundation of capitalism itself, which becomes no longer industrial but transnational and liberal, social and communicational. This new historical throws into crisis the framework that Karl Polanyi had outlined in the 1930s in terms of leaving behind the self-regulating market. In Dockès' view, we have rather to understand how irresistible are the contradictions opened by the formidable growth of the knowledge embedded in human capital, in the face of the financial power and juridical organisation of capitalism. Defined here is a new package of contradictions: between the freedom of immaterial labour and the need for it to be disciplined, between excedence and control. And this brings us, impressively, to the underlying reasons for the present crisis of production.

Through his contribution 'Finance Capitalism, Services and Knowledge', Patrick Dieuaide positions himself within this overall descriptive and critical account: financial capitalism and the stock markets are not to be seen as a parasitic dimension but a structural expression of the transformation of the spheres of production and exchange. The processes of value creation can no longer be identified in terms of the measurement of labour time but must rather be described by a logic based on the times of circulation of capital. The values that are formed on this new basis are guaranteed and assured through new methods of control and management: we are here on the edge of a definitive socialisation of the productive circuit of cognitive values, and therefore of the complete socialisation of the values produced. In the post-Fordist organisation of labour, crucially cooperation is the basis of the definition of productivity and its exploitation.

It is not by chance that Vercellone makes his second intervention, 'Transformations of the Concept of Productive Work and New Norms of Distribution', on this basis. The author seeks here to go beyond the standard approach to the concept of a 'guaranteed and adequate social income', which has hitherto remained locked in traditional approaches to the measurement and distribution of wealth. But, if the argument developed thus far has any value, we shall have to recognise that, in cognitive capitalism, the new image of social wealth is to be found in the profound changes that have affected both the concept and the reality of productive labour. Hence the 'guaranteed social income' will no longer be conceivable as a transfer income, offered on the basis of various sources of economic activity; on the contrary, it will be conceived as a primary income, directly determined by the social character of production. A collective social wage is now needed, which should be based on the recognition that the source of the wealth of nations and of the gains in productivity resides by now in the productive cooperation that takes place at the societal level. But this also means that the 'guaranteed social income' has to be matched to some kind of collective social output. It is clear that this logic of the socialisation of capital is a radical alternative to all the spurious socialisations that capital has invented, from the public limited company to the implementation of pension funds.

The article 'Cognitive Capitalism and New Forms of Codification of the Wage Relation' by Yann Moulier Boutang develops this line of thought very powerfully, despite its schematicism. The structural crisis of the canonical wage code, which was 'full time and of indefinite duration', and the transformation of wage labour into atypical and precarious forms of employment represent a profound and radical mutation in the capitalist mode of production. Analysing the context created by the new conditions of production, Moulier concludes that now not only does the formal structure of wage labour go beyond the remuneration of labour time, but also the new structure of the labour force has created big problems for any measurement of the wage. (Later on we shall see further consequences of Moulier's argument). So these five contributions, which I regard as the fundamental core of the book, develop the theme of general intellect by describing the scenario of a post-Fordist economy that not only fully realises the real subsumption of society to capital but also, by identifying the contradictions that this process creates, begins to describe the new consistency of cognitive labour and the new anthropological composition of the productive subjectivities. As we shall see shortly, this theoretical basis carries enormous consequences.

Second: some examples of critique of the tendency described thus far.

Anyone who has for years adhered to the thesis that Vercellone and the other authors develop here so persuasively knows the objections (now confirmed by decades of evidence) that are raised against this new perspective on capitalist development. Here, however, those objections become, so to speak, paradigmatic, and for this reason it would perhaps be interesting to address them, and offer a new critique of them.

I start with two articles, one by Geneviève Schméder, 'Breaks and Discontinuities of Labour in the Dynamic of the Division of Labour', and the other by Antonella Corsani, 'Cognitive Capitalism: The Impasses of Political Economy': they stand at two poles of an extreme (but not less effective on this account) opposition to the line of renewal outlined above. Geneviève Schméder argues for the continuing validity of approaches inspired by Adam Smith that focus on the essential relationship between the division of labour and the form and size of the markets. If one adopts the reading of Smith suggested by Allyn Young, the Smithian proposals are complicated and verified by joining together the rationalisation–fragmentation of labour and the social differentiation–proliferation of commodities and of industry. The division of labour between workers is therefore maintained and implemented by a division of labour between enterprises: the current changes in the cognitive economy are thus taken as indicating that the continuity of the logic of development of industrial capitalism triumphs in them. The linear continuity of this framework finds its opposite in the absolute discontinuity of the interpretative proposal offered by Antonella Corsani. Contrary to the view taken by Remy Herrera and Carlo Vercellone, Corsani argues that it is impossible to place a knowledge economy and an economy based on the cognitive development of production within the Marxian system. Scientific knowledge (and knowledge in general) cannot be reduced either to capital or to labour. The production of knowledge is an autonomous 'in itself and for itself'. It is given then as an independent sphere of capitalist accumulation. From this point of view, any attempt to relate back the paradigmatic rupture associated with the advent of cognitive capitalism to an endogenous reading of the emergence of a knowledge production within the industrial paradigm (whether within standard economic theory, within Marxian critique, or within Schumpeterian heterodoxy) is doomed to failure. As I said, the contradiction between Schméder and Corsani is total: the former argues for homogeneity, the latter argues for a metamorphosis in the process. I have no intention of addressing these theoretical oppositions in terms of the one cancelling out the other. However, there is no doubt that the historical reductionism of Schméder is based on an inability to relate to the new, and is similar to the idealistic creationism that Corsani claims to trace in the process. Both these authors lack an understanding of what is most characteristic to the point of view introduced and defended by Vercellone and his colleagues: the development, and especially the transformation, of the economic horizon derive from the class struggle, when the latter is qualified by the underlying contradiction or opposition between living labour and dead labour. The cadaverous continuity of Schméder finds an equivalent in the ethereal discontinuity of Corsani.

Of course, this is better than the stale repetition of orthodox (and sometimes third-worldist) models that minimise the transformations and consider as not only predominant, but obsessively repetitive and determining, a unilateral logic of capital that subordinates knowledge and strips of any originality the current economic horizon and the transfomations that take place in it – not to mention that it forges the technical and social division of labour along traditional lines, exclusively as a function of its exploitation. François Chesnais, 'Property Relations and Forms of Capture of the "Cognitive" for the Benefit of Financial Capitalism', and Claude Serfati, 'Finance Capitalism at the Centre of Contemporary Relations of Production', develop these arguments with an obstinacy matched only by their inability to grasp the most obvious changes in production today. Their arguments are all based on a belief that capital still maintains complete domination over the production of knowledge and over the transformations in the division of labour: both are seen as being still subject to a strictly Taylorist logic. At this point, of course, a number of catastrophist elements and nihilist consequence are added to the brew. For example, the massive orientation of scientific and technological research in postmodern capitalism, far from modifying the technical and political composition of production, is increasingly directed to military ends and to the appropriation–expropriation of the living [*del vivente*]. . . This serves to frighten the children, and summons up the bogeyman of a society in which cognitive capitalism triumphs, and so on.

I suggest that, when you consider this series of critical positions against the experience of innovation in the productive sphere and against the theory that tries to give an account of this innovation, perhaps Bernard Paulré has a point when, in the postscript to the book, he says that taking the question of the division of labour as the basic criterion in the description of the current economic and political situation may not be enough. He is right especially when, with a certain emotional rhetoric, he insists on the complexity of the issue and on the inconclusiveness of the attempts to analyse these transformations. Whereas Vercellone's book considers that an analytical and microeconomic approach to the current division of labour is enough to uncover the extent of the transformation and the global reconstruction of development, to Paulré it seems rather that the complexity of the system of production does not permit this step from the analytical to the global. With this in mind, he sides with the divergent interpretations of the evolution of the contemporary division of labour. And while it seems that both sides – both those who argue for changes in the paradigm of production and those who claim continuity in the new dominance of finance – may, despite their differences, eventually reach agreement on the fact that we are moving beyond industrial capitalism, this shared recognition does not shed sufficient light on the complexity of the situation. A conclusion couched in these terms (*à la* Baudrillard) demonstrates, or so it seems to me, the real difficulty and sometimes also the confusion that emerge when we seek to build a consistent picture of this stage in the political economy of capitalism.

Third: why the definition of a new economic era is not enough to define a new historical era.

When you read all the arguments developed in this book, you are left with a sense that the attempt to define a new economic era on the basis of a development of the 'fundamentals' of political economy is not enough to clarify what has really happened in today's economic and civil history. Perhaps, when we take into account the arguments for complexity that are printed here, rather than being reassured we are left wondering whether we are facing an implacable bias in reasoning. Economic policy and, all the more, political economy seem incapable of biting on the complexity of the connections that the real 'subsumption' of society to capitalism has created. Perhaps we should start talking about *the end of political economy*: in fact, the more production becomes socialised and globalised, the more economic science and its various attempts to define the measurement of labour and of development go into crisis. Given all the phenomena that this book assembles, it would probably be more useful if we returned to setting up inquiries [*fare inchiesta*] in the sense of going to seek the foundation of value in the *common* recomposition of labour and in the concrete *cooperation* of the subjects (both individuals and groups) who inhabit the world of production. But, if we do this, we shall no longer be able to find units for the measurement of labour. . . And what is the point of a science of economics, if it has no means of measuring? Even if we were to find them, these measuring units would show themselves rather as a random a posteriori arising from the common organisation of society and from the political solution, each time renewed, of the antagonisms that traverse it. So economic science should probably open itself definitively to political science or, to put it more clearly, should bow to political practice. Because, if anything has become clear here, it is that economic orthodoxies no longer exist and that the 'fundamentals' are always heterodox and spurious.

It should be said that the contributions of both Vercellone and Moulier Boutang point to these conclusions. The analysis of the characteristics of the production of value, in cognitive capitalism, defines new principles and offers a post-Smithian division of labour. Obviously in the present article I cannot go into a discussion of the nature of the new input–output matrix. It is enough to stress that this broad accumulation of arguments points clearly to the need for a new *tableau économique* and for a new, corresponding map of the structuring of public accounting. Indeed we can now see with increasing clarity that 'external economies' constitute the general conditions of development, investment and income distribution. At this point it is obvious that the question of 'citizen income' and all the modalities of social rights and labour rights that derive from it are internal to the economic discourse and represent a kind of constituent *dispositif* within it; but, for this very reason, that question defines itself increasingly as the element of a broader political science.

If one is to verify definitively the insufficiency of the economic approach within the new dimensions of social development, there remains one final argument. For some time historians, philosophers, sociologists and political scientists have grasped this overspilling from economics to politics and the new point of view situated between the two, the interaction that binds them together: they refer to it as *the biopolitical fabric of social analysis*. In my view, this element of the biopolitical is precisely what economics needs today. Vercellone's book, with the various subject headings it offers and the contradictory positions it invites in some of the conclusions it proposes, is clearly moving towards a biopolitical definition of a normative practice of the social.

5

From the Factory to the Metropolis

> The metropolis is to the multitude as, in the
> old days, the factory was to the working class.
> Reflections on an old saying and on some more
> recent experiences (of struggle)

> But the left does not understand. On the contrary: *il faut
> entendre le grondement de la bataille* [one needs to hear the
> rumble of battle]
>
> Foucault

From Left and from Right: The Expropriation of the Common (in Postmodernity)

There are too many old elements in the catastrophe of the European left, in the anticipation of the fall of the Berlin Wall and as a result of it; and we know what they are. They can usually be traced to an unchanging view of the social and political composition of classes. For traditional left-wingers, this view, for what it is worth, remains that of the Fordist worker and of the productive middle classes – and, increasingly of late, that of the middle classes, but with the addition of some new elements, such as the adoption of increasingly 'biopolitical' parameters for the evaluation of the social. People are beginning to realise the intensity with which political factors invest and constitute life itself, the production of wealth, and the reproduction of populations and how, in these determinations, politics should be held responsible. Biopolitics is that 'common' (sites of knowledge, metropolitan structures, languages and ways of life) that makes up a large part of our existence. The discourse of the new 'democratic party', in its ongoing and banal expressions, is characterised, in Blairite fashion, by the attempt to direct and control the violent process of biopolitical differentiation of the income structures that characterise liberal society. Our Italian 'democrats' are adapting to that model. Now, it is a fact that, when they appear, these new parameters are not there to affirm the 'common' but rather to dissolve it, not to grasp the new but to confound it. . . The problem of our left-wing democrats is that they no longer have any real reference points, whether social or of class, to which they should answer. The 'middle classes' have done justice to the 'socialised worker', for sure; but there is no one left to produce struggle from within this new perspective. The autonomy of the political, of the media, of the chattering classes has the upper hand. This is the state of the debate in the Democratic Party. We have to restore the biopolitical balance of the social. Is this a goal or a political stance? As regards the centre, no one could doubt at times that here we have a void, or even an abyss. In fact, if you ask them, the left-wing democrats, why they are doing this or that, they fall silent; and getting them to talk is like pulling out a tooth. The situation on the right is simpler: the right maintains its habitual class reference points and continues to pursue its customary objective of making investors richer, of exempting their fortunes from tax, and of offering them, in the gigantic market of privatisations, new possibilities to consolidate their wealth on the highest positions of power. This is how it is, but is it all? In the face of the inconsistent policy proposals of the democratic centre-left, the specificity of antidemocratic centre-right policies is characterised by the shared objective of establishing and strengthening a new property-owning elite. It feels like we are going back to the days of Louis Philippe. But it's not even this. Today the situation is very different and, while Berlusconi may be the stereotype of a clownish repetition of history, the right, the conservatives of today, really are not those of the times of Louis Philippe. These new businessmen sink their claws into that 'common' that the new organisation of living labour has built in the transition beyond the factory system, beyond Fordism. (And, for now, let me pass over the new 'reactionaries' of the left, who sometimes pose as *ultra-left-wing*, the kind of people for whom nothing has happened in the world: for them the bosses are always the same (and the proletarians too), the nation-state is always the messiah, and internationalism is a pernicious utopia; I shall return to them once the democrats of the left and those of the conservative right have been dealt with.)

Elements of Exploitation and Resistance Construct the Metropolitan Condition

But where are profits, rents, and wages today? Property, enclosures, power – where can these be recognised today? The answer to these questions – as proposed by a number of friends and comrades whose opinions I share – is located and centred in the metropolis. The metropolis is in fact the place where the epochal transformation of the characteristics of labour power has revealed itself and, consequently, where the threads of development and resistance knot themselves together. Labour has become a network of activities; value creation a cognitive process; and wealth the circulation of information – this is the metropolis, and it is a precondition of production. But there is something more (as the riots in the French *banlieues* have yet again confirmed): if the space of value creation, exploitation and exclusion has become a social space – precisely a metropolitan space, wherein class composition is going through radical changes – then the social struggles merge with this space and spread out over time and in the metropolitan project of liberating the multitude of the exploited. The contradictions, therefore – those of rent and profit, exclusion and capitalist exploitation – accumulate in the metropolitan area alongside the enormous productivity of labour. We had already begun to discuss this a long time ago, in the second half of the 1970s, when we understood for the first time that the factory system was definitively and unavoidably going to collapse and that the antagonisms were going to spread to the whole of society and would explode all the parameters of social discipline. At that stage we introduced the idea of the tendential hegemony of the 'socialised worker'. Today this transition is still under way, but we have a new series of understandings and passions. We understand that, when the factory system collapses, when production becomes social, reticulated and cognitive, when life itself is put into production, at that point the space of the metropolis is traversed by all the contradictions that the production of capital determines, encourages and mystifies. What applied previously in the factory now applies in the metropolis. The metropolis has become a huge melting pot of activities and exploitation: it is on the basis of an activity commensurate with this scale (and with the infinite virtualities that it contains) that the multitudinous proletariat moves in the metropolis. It is also on the basis of the new metropolitan contradictions that the bosses themselves move – trying to introduce systems of control over the metropolitan space that the new living labour has constructed and imposing, by means of enclosures, exclusions and hierarchies, the new model of an inertia that consolidates obedience to its command. Resistance, too, uses (this same) metropolitan space and is multiplied in that space.

The Metropolis Is Postmodernity, the Metropolis Is Globalisation

We think that we know what we are talking about when we say that the metropolis is the place where the contradictions and antagonisms of the new mode of production are accumulated. And yet this new and original reality remains quite unknown. The architects and planners give us complex images of what a metropolitan city is. Before addressing this complexity, however, let us agree on something that seems to me central: the contemporary metropolis is a *reality* completely *new* in the history of human cohabitation; and it is an *irreversible phenomenon*. By its very existence, the metropolis defines the postmodern. The metropolis exhibits an extreme and contradictory complexity but is always new; an intransitive novelty and an irreversible fact. There are scholars, both right and left, who consider that capitalist globalisation has been around for as long as capital has been; and they place it at the beginning of the Renaissance. However, this is not true: the globalisation of capital, in its present form, is an entirely new phenomenon. And, even if it were true that globalisation has been around for a long time, history has never known such an enormous accumulation of citizens and workers, of productive potential [*potenza*] and efficacy of power [*potere*] as we now have in the metropolis. Half the world's population lives there. Globalisation and the emergence of the large metropolitan structure are contemporary phenomena, born around and after the events of 1968. Consequently, all the systemic theories that considered the planet to be split into periphery–semi-periphery–periphery, between a first, a second and a third world – all these theories are definitely obsolete. And these theories have also brought about the end of illusions of a 'continuous' and 'balanced' development. Where are the hope and the theory of 'sustainable development' today? Where are the utopias of the 'glocal'? The space of the imperial multitude is metropolitan space, and metropolitan space is the space of the multitudinous antagonisms. *Hic Rhodus, hic salta* ['Here is Rhodes: jump here, then!'].

We Are at the End of the Transition from Fordism to Post-Fordism

If all this is true – in other words if it is true that in the metropolis the new mode of production and the new consistency of valorisation emerge from the concentration and accumulation of the living labour power of immaterial and cognitive labour (this is something that the centre-right and the centre-left have as a common position and enjoy) and if, in the metropolis, the flows of knowledge and understanding now act as an element of the common – then, as I have already said, all this means that the entire metropolitan dimension is traversed by the class struggle and that, within its flows and within the transformation that struggle brings about, the metropolis becomes the engine of the production of subjectivity. Hence it is both productive and antagonistic. This is what the left and the right do not find too enjoyable. Thirty years ago we set about analysing the diffuse productivity of the metropolis. At that time we had grasped the transition from the Fordist worker's resistance in the factory to the building of an independent reality of labour on the ground; and we did so by following the transition of workers from dependence on big factories to the autonomy of the industrial project. Small and medium industries integrated into local communities were at that time innovating the mode of production. We also grasped the change in the anthropological, social, technical and political composition of the proletarian subject. In any case, we concluded our analysis by asking for how much longer that fabric would be able to produce profit and to develop and when would it explode. When we discussed this web, we did not mean simply the development of a socially diffused industry; we meant the extension of the industrialisation of the social, in other words *the process of setting society to work*. Today we begin to have an answer to the questions asked at that time: if indeed that web were to explode, the productive socialisation (by capital) of the metropolitan web would not hold. This is what we are beginning to see today. The transition from Fordist production (the factory) to the post-Fordist system (metropolitan) is coming to an end – but the control systems that arise from this transformation are worn out. The transition has been made, but in the process of its actualisation it has consumed the tools and functions of command. The hierarchical and disciplinary mechanisms distributed throughout society now turn out to be unfit (or unsuitable or inadequate) for setting in motion increasingly different masses and variable multitudes of workers. The illusion of control over the metropolitan territory is shown (with all the force that an explosion can express) in the great revolt of the Parisian banlieue. This is not a phenomenon simply linked to processes of migration and assimilation and to their crisis, nor is it to do with phenomena associated with the shortcomings and the real inefficacy of processes of 'governance'. It is above all (not solely, obviously) a question of phenomena related to the disintegration of the metropolitan productive fabric, to the multiplication of cultural borders and of hybrid metamorphoses that take place at the end of the crisis of Fordism and right in the middle of the affirmation of the new cognitive mode of production. This crisis is a crisis of transition, powerful in its features, which deserves to be considered from a revolutionary angle. *But where is the left?*

Doing Multitude 'over the Metropolis': How?

It is clear that in the metropolis the multitude is subjected to processes of temporal discontinuity and spatial dispersion. It is in these conditions that the movements of the multitude clash continuously, on the metropolitan terrain, with the enemy. It is obvious that this happens. But how is it possible to unify – or rather recompose, retaining the difference among singularities – the multitude *against* the *dispositifs* of discontinuity and dispersion that it is constantly subjected to in the relations of production and in the political conflict that run through the metropolis? (This question can be related to the one that arises around the recomposition of subjects that are post-Fordist and cognitive, flexible and mobile. In fact discontinuity is, like flexibility, a *temporal* characteristic of action; dispersion is, like mobility, a *spatial* determination.) This is where the problem of 'making multitude' arises, in other words the problem of how to pass from resistance (or, if you prefer, from consisting phenomenologically in the multitude, from 'being multitude') to its political and constitutive dimension. In particular, it should be emphasised that the concept of multitude is a concept of a *set* of differences: an ontological concept, hence one posed *at a primary level*. The forms that are discontinuous (in time) or dispersed (in space), the differences of the multitude, will therefore appear as existential characteristics, as phenomenological modes, at a *level* that we may call *secondary*. In short, the concept of the multitude will always appear as the reality of a set of differences, whatever the discontinuities or dispersions to which the multitude is subjected. Important problems arise from this fact. Let us ask ourselves in particular this: How can one identify a communicative interface between the multitude as an ensemble of singularities and the temporal and spatial, recompositive and dissipative determinations of its emergence and of the metropolitan movements? And how can one describe these movements, classify or predict them – in what cycles, and according to what tendencies? A new *field* of investigation, or rather of *inquiry* [*inchiesta*], opens up here, but also a new field of classification and definition of historical periods. Because here we are dealing with a fundamental and definitive curvature of historical time.

Metropolis and the Biopolitical: From One to the Other

The problem is all the more important as capital itself, at this stage in its development, fails to offer us any coherent framework and thus cannot exert any capacity of command other than recourse to the state of exception. This, too (capitalist command, I mean), is overwhelmed by the discontinuity and dispersion of the dynamic elements of production, of the establishment of the common, and of the production of subjectivity. This is where the centre-left and the centre-right find the best part of a vague complicity between them. As they have no real alternative models, for both of them the alternative melts in the illusory and slightly drunken image of the glass that is half full and half empty. The homology between left and right in their conception of power (and I mean that both right and left think of power in the same way) renders the actors blind and indifferent. If power is considered to be formally homogeneous, for what reason, from the point of view of content, should it show difference? I said before that the democratic model adopted by the left (a model better placed beyond, to reform or erase the image of a society divided into classes) had the advantage of deepening and uncovering a number of biopolitical reference points: I added, however, that this model was adopted – whether consciously or not is of little importance – in order to confuse ideas rather than to open possibilities of developing resistance and struggle. For even the concept of biopolitics cannot but produce perverse effects, as long as we lack a new schema of intelligence and of promotion of the class struggle, as long as we do not assume the hegemony of immaterial labour – cognitive, intellectual, service, emotional and so on – over the entire production process, together with the assumption of the biopolitical model (I mean the will to spread over the whole of society the effects of rent, profit and wages, and thus the ability to think of them antagonistically at that level); as long as we lack this theoretical–political *dispositif*; and hence as long as the metropolis does not become the focal point of every description of postmodern exploitation, the place where one should hypothesise over any possibility of insurrection. The fact remains that capital is not capable of bringing about any kind of 'happy ending' for the future destiny of the metropolitan multitude, whether we talk about its financial and industrial or about its political capacities [*potenze*].

More on the Expropriation of the Common (in the Metropolis) and on the Birth of a (Metropolitan) Subject in Exodus

But, as we know, insurrection is not enough to bring about exodus. Rebellion is always beautiful, disobedience always useful – but today it is time for the multitudes to pack up and leave, with their flocks that feed them and their tents that protect them and their weapons that defend them. To rebel is right, but it is not enough. What is becoming decisive now, in this enormous transformation of human life in post-Fordism and globalisation, is *the production of a new subjectivity in the metropolis*. Which means that the analysis of the metropolitan production of subjectivity becomes fundamental here and now. I said earlier that the failure of the (democratic) left consisted in its inability to conceive of the new class structure within today's system of production, or within a production where the processes of valorisation have become increasingly immaterial and cognitive and (from a spatial point of view) overflow the metropolis and immerse themselves in it. The metropolis is the place of the hegemony of immaterial labour. The capitalist appropriation of cognitive surplus labour and the generalised exploitation of knowledge take place precisely in the metropolis. The metropolis is the point at which the cooperation and the networks extend to build an abundance of goods and relationships as well as of wealth. In the metropolis capital develops more advanced processes of appropriation. But then, in addition to this capture of labour and knowledge, other forms of capitalist appropriation join in: those that pass through taxation or are organised through the expropriation of public services, of common activities, of the social productive force that the metropolis expresses. It is in this area that the capitalist expropriation of cooperation in its postmodern aspect includes all the operations of impoverishment, exclusion and destruction of the welfare state. Exploitation thus extends in a general manner and occupies all the spaces of the social, including those of exclusion (which are necessary to the organisation and hierarchies of the metropolis). I could add at this point many other things that need thinking about, but just one will suffice, which is fundamental: it addresses metropolitan cooperation, in its general aspects, and the forms of wages. If production is social, the measure of the wage should take place within this social form. But this does not happen. Why not? Could capital sustain this relation of measurement (*social production equals social wage*) and the pressure that goes with it? In any case, this is where the *dispositifs* of discontinuity and dispersion of the multitude (as well as those of mobility and flexibility of labour) intersect with the strategic problem of social reproduction. Now, if when one speaks of the production of subjectivity one is talking of a production of subjectivity that derives from the metropolitan social fabric as a network of cooperative conditions, and if the multitude is a set of singularities, once it is recognised that these singularities (identified in the wage dimension) may recompose themselves in the common, we have to ask how this common can produce decision, struggle, and a will to revolutionary transformation.

The Multitude in the Metropolis

As you see, at this point I have no conclusion to propose. We simply have to deepen our awareness of being in the middle of a new path – or rather a new and irreducible problem, posed in order to *territorialise* the concept of *multitude*. Only through the territorialisation of the multitude can the time of singularities effectively open to historical virtuality, to events, and be studied as such. I would add that it is only when one territorialises the concept of multitude that all possible references to a consciousness 'external' to the movement fail and all claims to the universalisation of the project dissolve; and then a reappropriation of the material conditions and of the productions of subjectivities involved in the cooperation of singularities – a reappropriation adequate for this purpose – presents itself with force. It is a power [*potenza*] that is finally territorialised.

If you want at all costs to arrive at a conclusion, the only feasible one is that which research, or rather militant co-research, indicates. The thing is to determine, within the *dispositif* thus far only defined, how the multitude can situate and articulate itself within and in relation to the metropolis, without forgetting the way in which the working class used to place itself within and in relation to the factory (but at the same time forgetting it, of course). So what does it mean to talk of opening multitudinous struggles in neighbourhoods of the metropolis, on territories that come together in the metropolis? What does it mean to set territories to work for multitudinous subversion? One should admit that up until now only religious fanatics, who kill indiscriminately (in this they are the counterparts of state power), have succeeded in blocking the city. It is absurd – social struggles are side-lined and repressed, cancelled and mystified by terrorism and by the prevention of terrorism (the capitalist inability to find an end to the activity through accumulation is produced and demonstrated in the prevention of terrorism). So be aware: they are workers, those murdered bodies that block the city when the terrorist attacks. If we want to put them in a non-passive relation with these events, we need to reverse this situation and to prevent the workers' bodies from being presented as victims of terroristic bombs – as they had been before, for the cannons of the order established by the likes of Thiers and Bava Beccaris (only the Nazis wanted to close the circle between terror and order virtuously, and we know with what results). Today is the time for *active disobedience*, a simple forerunner of and introduction to multitudinous organisation for the conquest of the metropolis. I still have in my library the Third International book (edited by Palmiro Togliatti) on the insurrectional taking of the capital cities of nation-states: how to attack government buildings, the post office, the state radio, and all the headquarters of state and military agencies. This is no longer of any use today. There are no longer avant-gardes that could lead us towards the centres of power. On the other hand, the centres of power can be absorbed and dispersed in the multitude. The strikes of 1995–6 in Paris, the Argentine struggles of the first years of the new millennium, the great struggles around water issues and ecological conditions in India, and also the current ones in the Val di Susa: these teach us more about it than the theoreticians of insurrection ever did. Setting up the multitude against the metropolis means recognising that the metropolis is constituted by the common, it means imposing, by common and insurrectional means, the truth that only the multitude can make the metropolis live.

Multitude versus Metropolis

Between the working class and the multitude in struggle there are similarities, but above all there are differences. In the relationship between that similarity and diversity, the destiny of the multitude is gradually taking shape, precariously but nonetheless effectually. The multitude is a new name for the collective subject that undergoes and rebels against exploitation. The multitude has taken the place of the working class in producing and experiencing the pain of exploitation, as well as in resisting it. Today the multitude is defining the space of expression on which to inscribe the times of liberation from exploitation. But it is no coincidence that the passage of the revolutionary subject from the factory to the metropolis represents a metamorphosis for the subject itself: the intersection between spaces and times of liberation is not indifferent to the social and political composition of the subject. The 'fusion' that old Sartre pointed to when defining the working class in struggle and the process of realisation of communism to the point that the latter would dissolve itself, qua class fusion, in the struggle from the factory to the social – well, that fusion has further extended in space, and the dissolution of the factory as the central place of struggle has shifted its potentiality [*potenzialità*] onto new subjects and onto the new space of the metropolis. It is clear to all, at this point, how deep the blindness of both the right and the left is in the face of this metamorphosis. If, as I said at the start, neither the right nor the left knows how to get out of the model of appropriation of collective labour power, which is concentrated in a homologous – homogeneous – and compact idea of power, it will necessarily miss this singular transformation of time and space, and also the constitutive *dispositifs* of the multitude. Because the multitude, in occupying space, also determines its articulations, presents itself as a flow, as a collective and political entrepreneurship, as constituent power. It is no surprise that in these territorial spaces all the categories of political economy go into crisis. What is now the relation between profit, rent and wages? The monetary relation of exploitation is now completely arbitrary! What is the new definition of exploitation, no longer tied to the law of value but to the expropriation of common cooperation? What is now, and what will possibly be, the relationship between the political government of exploitation and movements of struggle in these new spaces, around these new torsions of multitudinarian and metropolitan living? The crises – be they financial or fiscal, of politics or of production – are now nothing other than *ontological crises* of living in common. So, when we address the problem of the relationship between the multitude and the metropolis, we are entering an entirely new territory by comparison with the traditional experience of revolution and the dynamics of the transformation on the basis of which we have acted thus far. In the previous section I recognised, in some of the great struggles that straddle the twentieth and the twenty-first century, new and exemplary characteristics with reference to what I am now discussing. These are new phenomena, of course, but also irreversible (and don't let the novelty mislead you: some people are hoping that this level will recede, but the newness of the event is, on the contrary, a formidable expression of an irreversible accumulation of struggles). 'Starting again from scratch does not mean turning back': this was always true, but it is true especially today, because those who start again from scratch – from the social and communist struggles for the transformation of this world – do so on the basis of an ontological transformation of the subject, of the times and of the space in which it is inscribed (and they do so on the basis of knowing that capital has become totally parasitic). The fact remains that this new destiny has to reveal a specific *kairos* and that this new composition must express a matching capacity for decision-making; the circle must be capable of turning itself into a straight line. To make myself better understood (although many pretend not to understand), I can say that there is a deep continuity between the struggles of the Parisian banlieue and those of, say, Val di Susa.

Topics of Inquiry

All of this opens some problems in relation to which the *militant metropolitan inquiry* should be developed. These are problems that directly affect the politics of the left, because they are radically innovative by comparison with the way in which the left governs the metropolis in Italy, Europe and the United States. Multitudinarian autonomy, if it expresses itself (as it expresses itself) in the metropolis, obviously raises programmatic issues that are fundamental at this point and take priority over all other political choices. One could say that these themes are of two kinds: one kind relates to the *socioeconomic* management of the metropolis and the other to the *sociopolitical* determinations of the government of the metropolis. As regards the former, there are two points that are closely related. One is the *attack on urban rent* as a basis for the creation of a metropolitan *citizenship income*. I mean that the destruction of urban rent could, even on its own, fund the financing of a basic citizen income. The second point of view involves the construction of a deep and irreversible relationship between *investment in production* and *investment in services* in the metropolis. The multitudinarian 'common' is built within this metropolitan economic relationship. This means that investments, private and public, should be essentially directed towards the expansion of metropolitan services, which from now are seen as the fundamental basis of any increase in productivity. A second set of problems, as mentioned above, concerns the government of the metropolis. This is where metropolitan autonomy has to be completely redefined, organised and taken up institutionally. The disarming of the police and the democratic–urban rooting of the judiciary (not to mention the control of both by the metropolitan self-government) have to be imposed. Alongside this there is the matter of building, within an appropriate constitutional language and an appropriate constitutional machine, an effective and democratic articulation of the relationship between multitudinarian autonomy of the metropolis and national government. There have been many experiences of possible relations between movements and governments in global governance. As the discussion proceeds, I should explore such issues. But, for the moment, the above will suffice.

Beyond Representation, Organising the Road to Exodus

One last question for discussion. It can be seen (depending on what answers we give) either as an appendix to what has already been said or as the indication of a new constituent path to be travelled. This question is: How do we locate *multitudinous power* [potenza] in relation to *political representation* – where the latter has the management of the metropolis in the framework set up by capitalist command? One thing seems immediately clear: the attack on urban rent, the preparation (or advance constitution) of a metropolitan fund for citizen income, a policy geared to creating investment in metropolitan services, and the construction of instruments of detailed research and of democratic governance for metropolitan self-government – these are all issues that cannot be put off. So either the structures of local government lend themselves to these urgent needs or they have to be forced. In the first case, the 'local' structures of the government of the metropolis (but we have already seen that these are not local) and the movements will organise themselves together to act outside of the central determinations of capitalist command; in the second case, those same structures (and the movements) will move *against* the current determinations of command and will seek new forms of legitimacy for their action, will want to build new tools of government. For me, the important thing is that the relationship between *outside* and *against* should always be obvious to the intelligence and the will of the singularities that are acting in the multitude. 'Outside' means that people know where to go, what the problems to be solved are, and what resources can be mobilised to build a society a little more decent than the one we currently inhabit. 'Against' means having understood the need and the forms in which one still acts *against* (and naturally within) the bourgeois society of the empire of capital. This is the relationship – between the against and the outside – that interests us: *a radical exodus*. Some call us utopians; perhaps we were, all those years ago, when we had not yet experienced the explosive force of the relationship between multitudinarian movements and governments (and all the other institutions of capital) that is established in 'governance'. Perhaps we were when, many years ago, we still saw the Communist Party as a revolutionary force and we entrusted it with our destiny, joining a struggle that was 'within and against'. Perhaps we were also utopians, on other occasions. But why accuse us of this today? For us, today, to be 'outside' of capitalism can be declined in thousands of modalities of the concrete, *biopolitical* possibilities of existence. Capitalism is now a boat of bosses who are tired and sick, a ship sailing with a yellow flag in troubled seas, a story of parasitism, corrupt families, and also defeats of many useless moralisers . . . It's over! It's really over! A gang of self-styled leftists, democrats, miserable bastards, wants to show (no longer even prove) the opposite. . . Go ahead! What a course it has in store for us! The trio of Berlusconi, Rutelli, D'Alema . . . What scandal, what misery? We are irremediably 'outside' of this blatant falsification of reality. 'Against' and 'outside': *against* as only the most radical rejection of the exploitation of the way of life in capitalism can be; and 'outside' as only the imagination to build a new world and the strong consciousness of doing so right now, of having ideas, allow us. So now we have to start, at this height in the project, to storm the citadel of metropolitan power. The battle is already unfolding, antlike, in the city – the possibility of revolutionising the world of capitalism starting from the metropolis really does not seem unrealistic. Either way, the desire to do so is irreversible.

★ ★ ★

This article begins with a discussion of the disastrous state of the politics of social democracy. It continues with an analysis of new forms of struggle that the multitudes express in the metropolis; and arrives at an initial outline of the themes of a multitudinarian autonomy that might be developed by movement agencies. It is just a beginning, but at the same time it proposes an agenda that needs to be discussed. Perhaps the usefulness of this article will consist simply in the fact of having indicated (and having insisted) that these problems – of the relationship between the multitude and the metropolis – are the sole and exclusive problems around which a new left politics can be developed – in other words the transformation of the common ways of life in the metropolis. These are central problems because now not only the (communist) objectives but also the (democratic) means need to be treated together. And in the metropolis of the multitude you cannot have the one without the other.

6

Metropolis and Multitude

Inquiry Notes on Precarity in Global Cities

Finally the sky has fallen to earth, in fact onto the metropolis. Since 2005, the part of humanity that lives in cities is for the first time bigger than the part that lives in the countryside. At the start of the twentieth century, only four metropolises had more than 1 million inhabitants; today 372 cities have more than 1 million inhabitants, and forty-five have more than 5 million. *But why has this happened? Because the city has become a site of production.* Invested by immaterial and cognitive labour, crossed by technological and financial flows, cities have become places of production: flows of understanding and knowledge accumulate there and form a common good. New classes assure the biopolitical functions of the metropolis, and all the agents of welfare are located there. With heightened violence, power attempts to segment this metropolitan body and to make it a place of competition. We would need to rewrite *Capital* to describe this reality: if industry, as a system of indefinitely renewed exploitation of individual labour, has now gone out of fashion, it is on to metropolitan labour that despotism and exploitation get discharged; but metropolitan labour today is cooperative – not individualisable any more. However, it becomes increasingly difficult to expropriate the metropolitan commons, and the segmentation of the multitude continually translates into a common force.

★ ★ ★

As a result of this exhaustion of individual exploitation there is then a new face of exploitation, a new course taken by political economy: *revenue* [la rendita] *takes the place of profit*, the price of rented space [*affitti*] and services [*servizi*] in the metropolis becomes a lever for the expropriation of the urban multitudes. The economies external to the factory (industrial services, the use of common goods, the structures of transport and communication and so on) are now fully absorbed by the command over production. Thus, through the reabsorption of all externalities, profit is transformed into revenue and revenue affirms itself as an exclusive horizon in economy. It took the metropolis to bring about this revolution in economics.

The life of citizens is entirely absorbed into the mechanism of production; in the metropolis citizenship is put to work; despotism and exploitation copulate, as Guy Debord already noted in *La Société du spectacle*. It's amusing to hear it said that – as *weak* postmoderns and *strong* neoliberals claim – whereas the industrial disciplinary space was a space of imitation, today the urban and peri-urban space becomes a space of choice, of consumption, of comparison, of knowledge, as if the futility and the randomness of consumption had replaced the necessity and the toil of production. In fact *the biopolitical regimes of labour* (which involves both workers and housewives, both teachers and pupils, both the new cognitive classes and the inhabitants of the banlieues [*i banlieusards*]) are absorbed and commanded in the structures of biopower. Command over the city is structured as command over life; times and spaces are ordered for production and consumption. How sweet and reassuring this life is – the abundance of goods, the ostentatiousness of resources, the tempting offerings of advertising! In the metropolis, the phlegm of the rich inhabitant of the bourgeois city of the olden days is now converted into a 'constraint into production' device for the poor consumer.

* * *

But this cannot be, because the city is anything but an inert reality. The metropolis is the place where immaterial labour can become hegemonic, since all forms of labour are present there, from the most wretched to the most developed. Metropolises are institutional millefeuilles that gather together, in the prism of globalisation, the totality of the passions that generate the common. *And now we see the rise of resistance in this global hub, in this universal suffering.* Still life. Something other than and different from a desperate and miserable existence is being constructed at the same time as the experience of production is being lived. The metropolitan encounter takes place at the very moment in which segmentation and separation are established. The frontiers fall as soon as they are imposed. When they resist, it is only in the name of a fleeting mobility – but this mobility, too, is recomposed in the ongoing translation of the different into the singular. The metropolis was supposed to be a site of domination; it is becoming a place of resistance. *Mutatis mutandis, in the metropolis the multitude stands in relation to power in the same way in which the working class rebelled in the factory.*

★ ★ ★

Presenting itself as resistance, *it is desire itself that arises in the metropolis* – from difference, from the unbearable tension between an inert and dominated reality and the virtual and multiple potentiality of productive life. The metropolis, which has encased everything inside it, which has become *the factory of the postmodern conditions of the reproduction of life, finds in itself an immense articulation of resistances, de la vie au-delà de la survie* [of life beyond survival]. There is no point in the metropolis that does not present itself simultaneously as stability and movement, as command and resistance.

But, for this to appear, it is necessary that, against the post-Fordist metropolis, against the capitalist command that runs through the structure of the city in order to put it to work, *quelque élément de la métropole en vienne à déclarer la guerre contre le maintien de l'état de survie* [some element of the metropolis should come there to declare war against the maintenance of the state of survival]. It is not enough that workers and citizens should feel themselves, in the metropolis, simultaneously *included in* and *excluded from* metropolitan cooperation, from the productive structure of the city. It is not enough that discontinuities and dispersions should generate differences and insubordination within spaces and times that power still controls and determines: power has the means to turn random and partial unifications into corporatisms or into juxtapositions, or to reduce them to experiences of pure defence. *La multitude comme conscience et comme lutte surgit dans l'antagonisme avec l'ordre qui la canalise, la réprime et l'exploite* [The multitude as consciousness and as struggle arises through antagonism with the order that channels, represses and exploits it]. The multitude that is scattering, lines of flight, disobedience and divergence is not able to turn all these elements inside out and tie them all together – however productive it may be – without *producing a decisive act*: a declaration of class war, precisely. When the people of the banlieues [*banlieusards*] rebel in the suburbs, when precarious and intermittent workers organise themselves against the divisions that the command of the metropolis imposes, this is a declaration of war. *What is politically common* has to be built and *can be built only through struggle*, through an act of becoming aware, through the decision to reappropriate the product of common labour. This is because *the metropolis is a result of the labour of the multitude and is the source of the will to power* [potenza] *of the multitude itself.*

* * *

Bear in mind that even this decision can abide illusion, even this power [*potenza*] can abide mystification. When they speak to us today of 'creative classes', for example, they are again speaking of separate logics of inclusion and exclusion. The future – they say – promises inventive labour, which would be the opposite of inertial and executive work. But the metropolis, we have seen, is a single territory: what is invented *est tout à la fois de l'ensemble commun et des individuals qu'il agence* [belongs at once to commonality and to the individuals it puts together]; in contrast, what is decided at the political and economic level, *in the sphere of biopower,* produces a common that is hierarchical – with effects aimed at increasing revenue and extended so as to exclude newcomers and the weak. Inequality in the metropolis speaks *une langue semblable à celle de* . . . [a language similar to that of . . .] *the very language of inequality in the factory*: it is an operation of exploitation that pretends to be a functional necessity. Fantasies about the 'creative class' – a debased metropolitan imagination, a miserable conscience – invent neighbourhoods in the metropolis that are open and happy, that invite urban tourism and continuous intrametropolitan 'raves'. In reality, these fantasies are in the service of real estate agencies – their real point is to make profit from the real estate speculations that follow the internal migrations in metropolises. But you have to know how to read inside these movements, to understand how metropolitan social spaces areas are in reality constructed by the many facets of desire and resistance. *Multitudinous power* [potenza] *does not bow to metropolitan biopower.*

This holds as long as war has been declared – to declare war is to know the metropolis – and as long as the war is lived within the asymmetry between biopolitical regimes of productive citizenship and structures of metropolitan biopower. *And the war of the multitude, in the asymmetrical regime of the metropolis, is an urban guerrilla war.*

* * *

The metropolis is a space of realisation of the common potentiality of the multitude, and this space cannot be realised starting from the centre, by giving it a single norm; only by working through the lines of segmentation and by intensifying them until they are all tied together can the decisive moment be determined. It is a question of constructing the common. Not reconstructing and not refinding it, but simply uncovering it as that construction that the various segments of the multitude put together day by day. Beneath command, against command, through a desire that is ever renewed, towards new conditions of freedom. *Beyond the private and the public, a metropolitan democracy of the common is thus given.* This is not something we find, or something we can easily institutionalise; it is something we live, it is a style or a way of life. The metropolis is a production of styles of life. But one should not confuse the individual lifestyle with the singular lifestyle that leads to the common and reassembles the multiple flows of production within a creative complex. Creative is only the *agencement collectif d'énonciation et de fabrication d'ensemble* [the collective organisation of enunciation and fabrication, taken together], only what functions as a transversal metropolitan machine. Jacobin legend has it that – once upon a time – there was a public (the muncipality, the state, the national, the popular, etc.). How much time had to pass before this illusion could be destroyed, or rather could self-destruct? For the public was nothing but the appropriation of the common by a transcendental aristocracy, by a mute and hard bureaucracy that put itself beyond the determinations and ruptures of the common singularities.

By contrast, the antagonism of the common reconstruction pursues and is coextensive with the metropolitan articulation, from the bottom to the top of the skyscrapers, from the 'outside' of the banlieues to the city centre: it is by pursuing these trajectories that antagonism can reconstruct the common. The common has no life except through the metropolitan transportations of citizens, the circulation of commodities and the information networks, the continuing exodus and the radical nomadism of labour power from or into the capital. Now, if the multitude is coextensive with the metropolis, if it makes the metropolis live as a reality of labour – yes, one that is dominated but that nevertheless turns all the wheels of the metropolitan machine – this happens because *the multitude lives the metropolis as biopolitical potentiality* [potenza] *in excess over the controlling capacities of the dominant institutions.* The metropolis of the bosses is the metropolis that seeks to exploit, to control, and to put to work all energy, completely. By contrast, the free value that resides in the multitude in the metropolis is rich and impossible to tame. Be careful, it can turn against itself in the absence of an adequate revolutionary force; in that case it becomes fascism. But, while the multitude may be ambivalent and may not always be politically aware of its power, but only of the threats that weigh upon it, this ambivalence is also a terrain of opening and of alternatives. Here intervene knowledge and decision, solidarity or love, and political institutions. Ambivalence suffers; suffering is never revolutionary; *what is revolutionary is only the excess*, or rather the excedence, the step beyond the limit: this is the element of imbalance that the multitude brings into the city and that multiplies a thousand times in the metropolis.

In this way the multiple frontiers and obstacles, fracture lines and walls often come to be considered interfaces that polarise relations rather than blockages to mobility and antagonism. The interface is a membrane that pulses under the counterbeat of two worlds, of two different regimes. The interface is a place of entry and exit, a place of conversion and translation of languages, of transformation of what goes in and what comes out. In the metropolis there is always a difference of levels, a fracture of rights, which constitutes both the blockage and the potentiality [*potenza*] of the productive forces. *What is new is the link between the forces of production and the relations of production, which here needs to be approached, dislodged from its biopolitical form, and rebuilt in revolutionary form. This is what I mean by the conscious production of the common.*

★ ★ ★

Here we meet (or clash with) the theorists of contemporary urbanistics – or rather with the illusion, nourished by urban reformism (in which the vast majority of those theorists recognise themselves), of understanding, and hence of planning the life of the metropolis – an old modernist reflex (essentially Fordist, even if we are now a long way from that belle époque). They delude themselves: rather than knowing the life of the metropolis, they end up replacing it with a mystified image and making it utopian. They seem like lost kittens or big blind cats (depending on the scale of the investments entrusted to them) as they fuss around in the life of the metropolis, on the job. They fail – but how could they succeed? Architectural and urbanist hypermodern reformism is content to *produce transparency* – lightweight materials, glass, softness . . . – and sometimes to fix a constructive line rather than go beyond a *random and formal horizon*. But how can this effort – oriented as it is to transparency but unable to achieve it (don't perhaps fashion and film play better with transparency?) – operate in a metropolis where different productive sectors, generic forms of exploitation, omnipotent and indirect taxations, and demographic disconnections combine chaotically? What transparency is there in these dimensions? It would take perhaps a little humility to admit the chaotic ambiguity of the situation in which urbanist action is immersed, and thus to 'offer clarity' rather than impose transparency. But no; and so, in the absence of transparency and of any possibility to construct it, one gives way to cynicism. Architectural postmodernism knows, for example, that the holy trinity 'income–profit–wage' is an archaeological stratification and, while it is true that sometimes it attacks it, in some way it inherits and reproduces it, being aware that it cannot destroy it. This is mystified impotence, inability to plan according to the *biopolitical needs* of the metropolitan multitudes . . . Well then, let's do what we can, let us adapt to the commodity world in the productive and exploited metropolis, and let's recognise our inability to extract ourselves from capitalist command! Planning is overwhelmed by a sense of helplessness; the recognition of chaos and of the perverse nature of the exploited urban space ends up in withdrawal from action. In fact *the sciences of the city have bowed to biopower*. We have to reverse this situation.

⋆ ⋆ ⋆

One might say that we should not complain too much. After all, at the centre of the modern city there was always a square where they burned witches and heretics. In the bourgeois city, prisons and courts, prominently located in the centre, promised jail or the gallows to all who broke the law. And places of command still remain in the managerial and executive centres of today's cities, although they are often monumental buildings or, increasingly, temples of consumption. The forms of life should never be rescued from domination; in fact they should always be subordinated to capitalist command, even at the surface level. Viewed in this light, the metropolis is horrible.

But the city, the metropolis, has become a factory. To pass through the city today is to pass through an immense factory. And yet, contrary to what happened in factories, where the toil of production intersected with the joy of the encounter and the pain of labour intersected with class consciousness, *solitude and the multitude live under one roof in the metropolis today*. The metropolis is 'constant capital' in action, and thus frenetic expropriation of labour power. At the same time, however, the metropolis is the place where intellectual capital and the common, both produced by labour, are set in tension with the multitude. *The postmodern metropolis is therefore a place of exploitation, but at the same time it constructs a terrain of exodus*. The hegemony of the cognitive multitude over the process of production can thus be built here, just as the communist movement had built the manual worker's hegemony in the factory. Is this only a hypothesis? Certainly, but herein lies the decision of those who love freedom. Today the outcome of any critique of the city is the definition of a fabric of struggle in which the multitude can move: *if the metropolis is against the multitude, the multitude has an irresistible tendency to conquer the metropolis – the multitude as metropolis.*

★ ★ ★

In this transformation the architects have never had a clear place. Very occasionally they made Beaubourg buildings – but that was '68! Generally they built Trump Towers. How can they redeem themselves? It is not my job to give lessons in architecture; but I can map the terrain and point out problems. If the metropolis is a productive terrain and if the whole productive relationship that involves the multitude is enacted there, then it will be necessary eventually to have, rather than an impossible transparency, a clear position and places of decision. Where do I place myself in order to open the *production flows* that traverse the metropolis, to bring about *possibilities of encounter* and of constructing struggles? There is no time left for foreclosures of resistance or for utopian flights. There is something that the architect, the movement of the architects, the collective architect, must above all pursue, taking the side of the multitude, in other words, opposing the invasion – which was first sporadic, then substantial – of urban areas by the so-called 'creative class' *à la* Tony Blair, and the 'gentrification' of the spaces of proletarian creativity. Second, one will have to try to structure communities with tendencies to exodus – communal housing, gardens and orchards for the many, multifunctional squats, cultural and political workshops, businesses of the common *Bildung*, and so on. The metropolitan multitude must be put in a position to organise itself, to recompose itself. Postmodernism, by responding to the needs of consumption, in some way permits this and solicits it: the new generations meet and hang out in the mall, in places of consumption and entertainment, with the same genuine naturalness with which older people reminisce about the parish or the gym. But by now the metropolitan multitude does not need that solicitation; rather it wants to move and breathe freely, to live in the centre of the metropolis and there to diversify and enliven metropolitan life. While the architects, having no illusions, entrust the city to the exercise of *biopower*, the point is, on the contrary, to return the metropolis to *biopolitical production*. This is how the multitude will be able to extract itself from the hell of expulsion, degradation and marginality and to recover the metropolis – as city – for transformations of life and for the exercise of democracy. Democracy also consists of the realisation of these spatial tasks, in the recovery of architecture for humanity.

Part II

Inventing the Common

7

Banlieue and City

A Philosophical View

Co-authored with Jean-Marie Vincent

We know that during the Industrial Revolution the banlieue took on a set of social, economic and political characteristics, and these characteristics grew particularly strong during the period of Fordism. And today we also know that, in the postindustrial era, the term 'banlieue' loses these working-class, industrial and 'red' connotations and comes to designate a series of dwelling places that form not towns but isolated conurbations or ghettos. The banlieue becomes synonymous with social problem; and the main actor in the question of working-class banlieues is no longer the proletariat, but rather the excluded. All this is certainly true for the most part, but does not apply solely to the banlieues.

The crisis of urban social relations affects not only the banlieues but the entirety of social relations and projects itself onto cities in a manner that is diffuse and often dramatic. In the 1970s the literature on urbanistics, and especially Henri Lefebvre, was already discussing the explosion of the city under the pressure of the capitalist reorganisation of territory and the deleterious effects of urban policies on the fabric of social and productive articulations that had constituted the wealth of the city. Our present task is to deepen our understanding of the relationship between the crisis of the city and the crisis of the territory, with particular reference to the banlieue. As noted above, both in the cities and in the banlieues the factors of destruction of the old structures of production coexit with the factors of construction of new networks of communication, production and circulation. Cities contain pockets of deep poverty, of new poverty, and between the dualism of the labour market and the social apartheid it is possible to identify new marginal layers.

Whether in cities or in the banlieues, the problem is the same. It is the crisis of a social bond that had been based on the productive order of the Industrial Revolution, which is now on the road to extinction, and thus the crisis of a certain figure of civil society that had been hegemonic in the course of the nineteenth and twentieth centuries. Put another way, the territorial, and in fact functional, separation of the city from the banlieues is inherent in the disciplinary processes of industrial society throughout the period of its development, and the collapse of this separation is the first explicit consequence of the passage from a disciplinary society to a society of control.

Thus we take on board the definition of contemporary metropolitan space furnished by Foucault and Deleuze, observing it through the categories of political philosophy.

As Deleuze says, whoever imagines that one is following in Foucault's footsteps by interpreting our society as a disciplinary society has misunderstood his thought. In essence, power no longer works through disciplinary *dispositifs*, but rather through networks of control. The definition that Foucault gives of disciplinary systems is a historical one. Before the supremacy of disciplinary societies, it was sovereignty societies that provided the model of domination; now, after disciplinary societies, control societies come to the fore.

Disciplinary societies are characterised by 'confinements' ['*reclusioni*'] or by institutions that constitute the scaffolding of civil society; these 'confinements' define the striations of social space. During its previous phase – namely during the phase of its sovereignty – the state kept a certain distance or autonomy from social production, manifesting its domination through the taxation of production, for instance; but in disciplinary societies the state supresses any distance and integrates or subsumes social production by means of organising the conditions of production. From this perspective, the factory is the paradigmatic 'confinement' in civil society. The disciplinary *dispositifs* that constitute the factory simultaneously subjugate and subjectivise the factory worker, turning the factory into a place of domination and resistance. The factory-like striation of society provides the state with a network for the organisation and coordinated striations defined by the institutions of civil society branch out in social space and create structured networks similar to the tunnels dug up by a mole. Gramsci had used the same image, only in military terms: 'the superstructures of civil society', he wrote, 'are like the trench systems of modern

warfare'.* Whether lines of power or lines of resistance, the striations of civil society are the framework that defines and supports the
social body. Today, however, these 'confinements' and these social
institutions are everywhere in crisis. One could perhaps interpret the
crisis of the factories, of the family, of the church, and of all other
social 'confinements' as the gradual erosion of different walls, which
leaves a social vacuum, as if the striated social space of civil society
had been smoothed out into an open and free space. However, one
of the most important lessons from Foucault is that power never
leaves a vacuum; on the contrary, it always fills empty space. This
is why Deleuze proposes that we see the fall of the walls erected by
the 'confinements' not as a process of social evacuation but rather
as a generalisation to the whole of society of logics that until now
functioned in limited spaces, where they propagated like a virus.
The capitalist logic perfected in the factories now invests all forms
of social production. This is true for schools, families and prisons,
just as it is for hospitals and for all other disciplinary institutions.
'Prison', says Foucault, 'begins well before its doors. It begins as
soon as you leave your house.'† Social space is smooth not in the
sense of being empty, cleared of disciplinary striations, but rather in
the sense that these striations have spread to the whole of society.
Social space has not been emptied of its disciplinary institutions but
filled with modules of control. The relationship between society and
state no longer involves the mediation and organisation of institutions for disciplining and dominating; it is rather the case that the
state branches out into the infinite circuits of social production.

However, the transition from a disciplinary society to a control
society is not simply a transformation or reorganisation of the structure of institutional domination. Foucault insists that institutions,
as a source of power relations, do not hold a predominant position.
Rather they represent the precipitate or the *dispositif* of strategies of
power. What works from premise and is put into action in institutions
is the diagram: the abstract or anonymous machine of strategy, the
non-formed or non-striated schema of power relations. In the transition to a control society, therefore, apart from the symptoms on an
institutional scale, we must grasp the configurations at the level of the

---

* Translator's note: *Selections from the Prison Notebooks of Antonio Gramsci*, ed.
and trans. Quintin Hoare and Geoffrey Nowell Smith (London: Lawrence and
Wishart, 1971), p. 235 (spelling slightly modified).
† Translator's note: Michel Foucault, 'Le Prison partout' [1991], in idem, *Dits
et écrits* (Paris: Gallimard, 1994), vol. 2: 194.

diagram. Put another way, we must first ask: What are the diagrams that define the conditions of the possible in societies of control? And, next: In what concatenations are these diagrammatic forces strengthened, and how?

The metaphors at our disposal no longer offer a possible approach to the nature of this transition. We cannot, for example, use the metaphor of structure and superstructure, which was so central to the conception of the mediating institutions of civil society. Not even the image of mole tunnels that characterised the structures of disciplinary society is valid in this case: it is not the structured pathways of the mole, says Deleuze, but the infinite undulations of the snake that characterise the smooth space of control societies. The metaphorical space of the control society is more plausibly characterised by the shifting shapes of desert sand, where positions are continuously displaced; or, better, by the smooth surfaces of 'cyberspace', with its infinitely programmable flows of codes and information.

These new metaphors suggest a significant shift as regards the diagram of the control society. The panopticon, and the disciplinary diagram in general, functioned mainly in terms of positions, of fixed points and of identities. Foucault was aware that the production of identities (even 'oppositional' or 'deviant' identities such as the factory worker or the homosexual) was fundamental to the functioning of domination in disciplinary societies. The diagram of control, however, is not oriented towards position or identity, but rather towards mobility and anonymity. This diagram functions on the basis of 'anyone' and therefore its provisions or institutions are developed primarily on the basis of the distribution and production of simulacra. The Fordist and Taylorist production of past years developed a model of interchangeability, but this interchangeability was based on common roles, fixed positions and component parts. The delimited identity of each piece and of each role was precisely what made the interchangeability possible. The production model of 'anyone' (in other words, of post-Fordism) offers a wider mobility and a flexibility that no longer fixes identities, and thus makes room for repetition. This is how controls over the most sophisticated flows of information and communication, innovative techniques for surveying and monitoring, and a wider social role for the media emerge at the centre of the functioning of power. Control functions at the level of make-believe in society. Anonymity and the [idea of] anyone in control societies are precisely the things that give them a smooth appearance.

Of course we should not misuse these metaphors by attaching an absolute value to them. To assert that civil society is in decline does not mean that the mechanisms of organisation and domination that characterise civil society do not work or no longer exist. In addition, recognising the transition from disciplinary societies to control societies does not mean that the disciplinary mechanisms and the potentials for resistance have completely disappeared. What is more, the fact that social space becomes smooth does not mean that there are no social striations; on the contrary, as Deleuze and Guattari tell us, in the smoothing process there reappear elements of striation carried to 'an unequaled point of perfection'.* In other words, in a certain sense, the crisis or decline of the 'confinements' or institutions of civil society gives rise to a *hypersegmentation of society*. For example, while for the past twenty years industrial production has been in decline and the social striation that defines it has been proceeding smoothly, this space is being filled, at least in part, by flexible forms of production that segment the labour force in extreme forms, creating mobile and anonymous networks of work done at home, of part-time work and of various forms of undeclared and semi-legal work. Paradoxically, the shift of industrial production to flexible production organises and confuses the smoothing and the hypersegmentation of social space. The new segmentation is extreme, but also flexible and mobile: we find ourselves in this way with the paradox of a flexible rigidity.

As for ourselves, we would like to start with the construction of new diagrams that can help us understand, at once, both the processes that smooth the social and the territory and those that segment it – or, rather, both the processes that unite the city and the banlieues and those that segment afresh, and deeply, this unified space. Indeed, only if we manage to interpret the effects of this new dialectic of the social and the political shall we also be able – by looking at things from the perspective of the predominant diagram – to identify the actors and instruments eventually capable of setting in motion a process of liberation.

1 Banlieues and Labour: A Sociological Perspective

To understand what is happening in the urban fabric of disadvantaged banlieues, it is not enough to study behaviours or attitudes; you also have to be able to understand in detail the social stratification

---

* Translator's note: Gilles Deleuze and Félix Guattari, *A Thousand Plateaus*. London and New York: Continuum Books, 1987, p. 543.

that predominates there, in other words the extraordinary tangle of differentiated social strata, of intergenerational relationships and of communication networks that structure social relations. An analysis in the traditional terms of class or socio-professional composition is not an option if you want to do this, because it has the disadvantage of missing a lot of key data, especially cultural ones. This is even more true in an urban fabric like that of Seine Saint-Denis (taken here as a paradigm), where the old forces of encadrement, integration and homogeneity that were represented by the Communist Party and the CGT until a few years ago no longer exist. The habitus have changed a lot as matrices of behaviours, the systems of representation have diversified, and the schemata of interpretation of social reality have been transformed. To speak in the language of phenomenological sociology, one could say that the lived social world of groups and individuals is in a state of radical change.

It therefore seems necessary to conduct analyses in terms of environments characterised by specific attitudes and formed around shared practices. In such a framework, history is obviously a very important dimension; it manifests itself in the historicity of behaviours and cultural formations. In other words, we have to be able to understand collective responses to given situations and contexts on the basis of a set of symbolic and cultural resources. Obviously we can ignore the effects of economic relations and of their conjunctural modulations (prosperity, unemployment, economic destructuring), but these effects are always publicised by the lived social world, by the capacities of groups to confront problems starting from their cultural baggage and practical traditions. In particular, we have to see how certain circles (a relatively homogeneous set of groups in interaction) can be destabilised in some situations (unemployment, for instance) while others are not. In some cases the lived social world remains stable and shows itself capable of absorbing contextual changes; in other cases it is destabilised and may even disintegrate. In fact there are continuous structurings and destructurings of environments, which involve changes in behaviours and in the patterns of interpreting social reality.

In the phenomena of structuring, great importance must be accorded to the relations between the generations and to the desynchronisation that we observe between their experiences and the creation of their respective lived social worlds (knowledge, schemata of interpretation, cultural values and so on). Some traditions are certainly passed on, but they are reinterpreted and changed, which means that the subcultures of those enviroments are constantly shifting. From this perspective, it is interesting to note that differences often crystallise around issues of leisure or around attitudes related to work. A survey like that of Rainer Zoll (*Nicht so, wie unsere Eltern / Not like Our Elders*) shows that a kind of cultural revolution is under way right now: young people from popular circles are characterised by the search for some expressivity in their lives outside work and in their leisure activities and by the avoidance of work that is too heteronomous in their professional lives. One can also observe in them new attitudes to militancy or to membership of political and trade union organisations. Young people enter organisations less and less, as if they were entering a religion. Their activism is often intermittent and depends on problems that arise at particular points in their lives. They mobilise when the stakes seem worth fighting for; they do not mobilise when, in their view, the stakes are not relevant.

Changes in the social relations between genders are also part of this context of cultural transformations. The number of young women who step out of traditional female roles, particularly that of the woman as housekeeper, is on the rise. Certainly domestic tasks and child-raising still rely on women, but this does not prevent them from seeking possibilities of autonomy and self-realisation in professional work and within couples. In reality they no longer assure the transmission of old family values and thereby weaken relationships of authority in society as a whole. At the same time they convey, at least in embryonic form, new concepts of human relationships, less marked by relations of power and domination. From this perspective, young women play a very important role in what Rainer Zoll calls the 'new individualism', an individualism that does not exclude the search for multiple communications and exchanges, even when they are difficult and precarious. As has been shown in all the studies carried out in France and Germany, most of the young women who are trying to restructure social relationships in order to be able to develop more freely seem to be very far from conservative positions.

On the whole, people over the age of forty-five do not accept these cultural changes easily; but they have no way of opposing them with their own culture, which is in turn disintegrating. In its communist or socialist form (social democratic in the case of Germany), this culture was organised, at the political level, around practices of social promotion and reforms of society centred on the welfare state. When, at the end of the 1970s, the welfare state began to face increasing difficulties (particularly around the funding of its activities and of social protection), this culture seemed to lose relevance, since prospects of social reform and full employment become seemingly impossible. So this old culture survives only in the form of nostalgia or of dogged protest, or in the form of attachment to organisational relationships (for example, the trade union as a way of life). This feels all the more ineffective as the collapse of the countries in Eastern Europe and of statist 'real socialism' comes on top of the recurrent crisis of the welfare state. There is, then, a predominance of backward-looking or defensive reactions among older generations in the face of a confusing and disturbing reality. The old working-class culture turns in on itself, waiting for better days that are never going to come. And so the younger generations do not have the option of measuring themselves against a strong cultural tradition, reinterpreting it in the light of their own experiences. They find themselves facing a fragmented tradition en route to exhaustion, which seems to have no relationship with their lived social world and the schemata of interpreting reality that these generations are able to develop. This prompts a great deal of uncertainty about the image they build of themselves. For young people, the current society is always marked by fundamental social inequalities; but its future seems neither clear nor readable. In this sense, for many young people politics is no longer a privileged instrument for transforming their situation and their way of life; it is just a set of institutionalised practices in which they get involved when they expect to be able to obtain concrete results. They are a long way from the ritualised and repetitive practices propagated by the major mass parties that, until relatively recently, dominated the political scene for the working classes.

By the same token, the massive nature of unemployment among young people under the age of twenty-five, the precarisation of work relations for many of them, and the extension of adolescence as a result of spending more and more time in systems of education and training make it difficult for a new culture to crystallise, fully formed and relatively unitary. Unemployed young people have difficulty in deciding which opponents they ought to fight and, as we have already seen, in defining principles of action; and this very often prevents them from giving themselves specific targets and finding positive points of reference. This means that many young people absorb rather passively the cultural changes that are taking place. They often prove incapable of reflecting about what they are doing. This gives great importance to the phenomenon of gangs. Very often denounced as a factor of delinquency and crime, gangs are actually places of refuge through which young people attempt to find ways to cope with an outside world perceived as hostile (which produces 'dregs'). They also try to build links of solidarity between them and to develop various means of expression (rock bands, dance, sport and so on). As Dubet has shown, there are positive elements that should not be ignored by focusing only on the aggression and violence associated with gangs. The violence of gangs and their links with drug abuse and drug trafficking arise from the fact that some young people are not able to master the problems that trouble them. Other young people who often come from the same environments respond in other ways, especially by investing in the academic system to avoid educational failure. From this point of view one has to take high school mobilisations very seriously.

All these things make it clear that the cultural changes under way are unavoidably ambivalent: they oscillate between prospects of transformation in social relationships and prospects of disintegration of the old social bonds. The cultural revolution under way – the aspiration for greater autonomy for individuals and social groups, the aspiration for a complex, rich and flexible use of human connections – clashes with the phenomena of exclusion, social marginalisation, and isolation in the circuits of social welfare. But, having made this observation, we should avoid falling into overschematic views on the two-speed society (in French terminology) or the two-thirds society (in German terminology). Strictly speaking we have not arrived at a degree zero of the social (except in extreme cases, the trends towards a disintegration of social relations are always countered one way or another by various and variously effective institutions). Thus we observe among the unemployed, young and old alike, often very ingenious attempts to combine assistance for the unemployed in its various forms (unemployment benefits, social remediation of unemployment, retraining courses, etc.) with work in the black economy, income-generating activities of various kinds, social activities, and so on.

In this respect we have to break with the excessively miserabilist and very often paternalistic and contemptuous representations of the disadvantaged environments of the large banlieues that are generated in knee-jerk fashion by the media and by some of those who have to deal with these problems. Those who are socially vilified and devalued as elements with very little to contribute to society have to get over a social handicap that probably weighs as heavily as any material handicap. Research in this area therefore needs to challenge these knee-jerk representations and to publicise as widely as possible the results that contradict the too easily dominant discourses. In particular, one should highlight the not insignificant reach of everyday solidarities, which are organised through informal networks, various associations, migrant groups, and the like. Of course, there are always families (often single-parent ones) and individuals who succumb in this struggle for social survival and dignity, but it is not from this point that the problems of the recomposition of social relations and the struggle against social alienation can be confronted.

There is no solution to the rampant crisis of the banlieues outside the emergence of new forms of social integration. Public policies can perhaps contribute (in particular fighting school dropout, rehousing the homeless, developing vocational training, and so on), but they will not be enough, because in the near future they will not have enough resources, either at the national level or at the European level, to do away with unemployment. Besides, we need to recognise that they cannot make up for the weakening of traditional forms of organisation and representation, either socially or politically. So one should ask whether there are not, at least in principle, new methods of aggregation for bringing together social circles that are scattered on account of their positioning and their social experiences. Paradoxically, the threat of unemployment, which spreads today to circles hitherto unaffected by it – such as the new salaried middle classes or workers in high-tech industries – could become a unifying element. Specifically, the scarcity of job offers, having become a constitutive and permanent part of the wage relation, forces more and more people to look into the matter of the division of labour and of what should be the place of work in life. Despite the not inconsiderable inequalities in access to work (particularly for reasons of cultural baggage), we can assume that representation (as mise-en-scène and as a phenomenon of delegation) will not be able to hinge on the valorisation of employed wage labour for much longer but will revolve more and more around questions of division and social use of labour.

We can even go further in this direction, because work understood as employment in a waged context is undergoing profound changes today. First, it is less and less a Taylorist kind of work (even if some branches of the economy are still dominated by Taylorism), and is increasingly a kind of work in which autonomy and intelligence play a major role. As Yves Clot has shown very well (*Le travail entre activité et subjectivité*, PhD thesis, Aix-Marseille 1, 1992), the use of workers' subjectivity is an essential element in the most modern processes of production. To ensure continuous and flexible production, workers have to be involved in micro decision-making, whereas from macro decisions and the bulk of the organisation of labour they remain excluded.

Workers are called upon to realise a maximum of subjective investment, but at the same time they are denied the means of achieving it completely. There may thus be both subjective investment and subjective counterinvestment. So the exercise of the capacity for work occurs in conditions of attraction and repulsion that make it problematic and quite contradictory. There is, in short, a point of contact between a latent crisis of the social division of labour (the sharing of work in society) and a latent crisis of the division of labour in companies (in the modalities of labour use).

2   New Networks and New Territorialisations: In Progress. . .

So the analysis cannot stop at defining the general context. Rather we shall try to show, mainly through the study of the banlieues, how – in the very places where the processes of destruction of the old solidarities and of the old conditions of living, work and communication are at their most advanced – we are witnessing precisely the emergence of new forms of social communities and work. During the past decade the studies devoted to this subject have been numerous and the interest aroused by the new productive and social structures that are taking shape in banlieue areas has proved to be very marked.

When we look at these processes from the point of view of the history of industrial development, things become much clearer. Especially when it comes to the destruction of old industrial zones, we are witnessing a process of decentralisation of productive activities that is particularly pronounced in the banlieues. Gradually, however, this decentralisation gives way to spontaneous processes of reindustrialisation: the decentralisation of major industries is matched by the growth of a complex network of small and medium enterprises in industry and in the service sector. It is in the context of this growth that new urban territories begin to define themselves. In anarchic fashion and without any guiding principle, the banlieue becomes the scene of a vast movement of reindustrialisation. The space of the banlieue is transformed by the continuum of production: the social, despite its disorder, contains an implicit order, defined by the new networks of mobility of labour, goods and information. From within the disorder of the new industrialisation there appears the socialisation of production relations, so that it is not easy to know what is the independent variable that keeps the movement in tension and in expansion: Is it still the ability of industry to invest in new areas in order to enlarge its own development project? Or is it, on the contrary, the pulsations taken forward by the networks of production, of the mobile and flexible workforce, of information, as they seek to centre themselves?

It is above all on this positive ambiguity that the analysis needs to focus. The Manichean positions that try to explain everything as being under the control of capitalist companies (a new 'Monopolville' in the context of the social diffusion of production) are just as groundless as those that look at the new horizon of productive networks from the perspective of a renewed Proudhonism. Our eyes have rather to capture a few more times the interaction between entrepreneurial strategies and the consolidation of territorial networks. This interaction consolidates the new realities of exploiting new territories; it reterritorialises flows and deterritorialises infrastructures. The process gives no sign of crystallisation; ambiguity threatens to recur all the time. An attentive analysis reads this ambiguity as the new normality of the cycle of production, over the long term.

The banlieue, as we said previously, is central to this development. It is here that the interweaving of new social and productive relationships has come about with the greatest dynamism. This is why post-Fordism places the banlieue at the centre of urban concerns rather than at the centre of industrial concerns (as Fordism did). The city – Max Weber's city, where the intertwining of production and social reproduction activities, of functional efficiency and cultural concentration represented the pinnacle of productive development, cooperation and command – is now to be found in the banlieues. Industry has finally returned to the city, but that city is now called banlieue.

It is not only in old Europe that the economic, social and urban sciences have remained silent in the face of this development: in the United States too, where these phenomena have at least ten years of pioneering, the debate has not made much progress and the crisis of the urban economy has been pinned on the productive growth of the banlieues, while the socialisation of production has been seen more as a conjunctural outcome than as an underlying tendency. The considerable problems caused by this transformation in the economic, social and urban field have been shifted towards the issue of getting over the crisis rather than oriented towards a theory of crisis as production of new social and productive decisions.

Even when the most striking point of the transformations is addressed, namely the tendential hegemony of immaterial labour in the new system of production, the analysis is more concerned with the technological determinations that create this new hegemony (the extensiveness of computerised networks, the expansion of personal computer use, the rules of production dictated by the computer) rather than attempting to understand the new nature of labour power, the new forms of its territorialisation, and the new aspects of the clash between city and banlieue on the one hand and, on the other, the new productive forces brought into being by this ensemble of processes.

So, by way of example, we could cite the extent to which the frenetic activity of urban research during the decade of socialist government in France showed itself unable to understand the novelty of the urban situation. Putting an end to the sectoral functionalism of the previous urban administrative activity, the documents that publicise the socialist policy for the city propose a systemic analysis of the city-banlieue as a whole, the complexity of the forces present, the need to understand the dynamics of these forces and to push them towards new experiments in social bonding and contract, and an active participation in the administrative and political process. So this was a correct interpretation of the new reality of urban social development, a radical critique of functionalist subdivision, and a big push for a comprehensive approach that should address problems from the bottom up (through associations and decentralised contracts with local government institutions). But this listening (and these timid suggestions for interventions) foundered in the encounter with reality, because of their inability to understand the *new productive nature of the urban territory*.

The radical questioning of state intervention in the city and in the banlieues, the sensitivity to the common problem that derived from this, and the requirement to make social citizenship the base and active presupposition of political citizenship were never rooted in an analysis of the fabric of production. Obliged to give a political and social response to the Minguettes riot in 1981, our warriors had terminated their experiment by the time of the Vaulx-en-Velin riot in 1990! But this failure was inevitable. Never, in fact, did city policy touch on or address the question of enterprise policy, never did citizenship policy intersect with industrial policy – except to brandish ridiculous notions such as 'citizenship in the enterprise'. Experimentation (the magic word of urban policy in the 1980s) thus found 'complexity' not as the basis for an intervention capable of achieving the productive presuppositions of social life, but as an ambiguous and chaotic whole into which one could disperse the residual capacities of militantism that had emerged from the end of the 1970s (in the course of a laborious but nonetheless realistic evaluation of the relationship between the productive, the social and the political).

3 . . . and in Crisis (Social and Political)

The complexity of the problems was, and continues to be, a matter of research. Sometimes it is constructed in devious ways, the better to avoid the central issue, the knot [*nodo*] of the crisis. *Complexity against the knot.* So what is the knot or crux of the crisis? It consists essentially in the fact that transformations in the structure of industry have broken the societal bond, they have eliminated the conditions of social cohesion – something that comes about and reforms itself continuously. They have prevented the operation of the old mechanisms of representation and institutional compromise. If this is the general problem of capitalist societies at the present stage of their development, it has become (if possible) even more acute and dramatic in relation to the new metropolitan areas (including cities and banlieues). Here indeed, in the banlieue and in the town, the relationship between citizens and administration has been sorely tested. The problem of the transformations in the mode of production appears in metropolitan areas amplified by a multiplication of the effects produced by the international dimension of those transformations. The crisis of ideologies, and especially the effects of destabilisation due to substantial phenomena of migration (both domestic and international), with the uncontrollable mobility of labour power that follows from them, have seriously and permanently redefined the social and political horizon. The radical transformation in the mode of production has brought the third world into the industrialised world, and it is within the metropolitan area that these two now face each other. The social and political composition of the working masses has been fundamentally transformed. The old forms of representation have been completely annihilated by these gigantic transformations. What apparently and above all should be the specific role of the administration (the transmission of information as a basis for decisions to be taken and as an efficient coding of rhythms of intervention) is now radically brought into question.

It is in this context that the three major crises of urban society are defined: first, the crisis due to the problem of exclusion; then the crisis related to the issue of citizenship; and, finally, the problem of participation.

In the light of what we have said so far, the problem of exclusion is the one that can be addressed most easily. It is the subject of a vast literature. It is the exclusion of all those who have been left behind by technological development; it is the worsening in the condition of those who are on welfare; it is the marginalisation of large sections of young proletarians; it is the obstruction of the social processes related to women's emancipation; it is the situation of immigrants who succeed in entering into the circuit of production only at the price of renouncing their rights. From the perspective of development, analysing the problem of exclusion means drawing the consequences from the analysis of changes in the most disadvantaged social strata. A 'two-speed society', that is what the current development model of the mode of production is proposing, insofar as it does not accord the same dignity to all those who participate in the social organisation of production. In the metropolitan configuration of development, the two-speed society presents itself in the form of a cohabitation between city and ghetto, between the modernisation of living spaces and the ongoing reality of old urban areas in a state of decay. Disciplinary striations mark the smooth surfaces of the postmodern city. In this horizon the problems of exclusion often become those of poverty or those of police repression each time when resistance appears, desperately and inevitably calling for an ever stronger repression. It is at the frontiers of exclusion, especially where the repression is most severe, that exclusion becomes illegality and behaviours become criminality.

As regards the issue of citizenship, analysis and rhetoric have played in equal measure. The fact is that, where social citizenship is non-egalitarian, the pretence of extending political citizenship rights in the same way is at best an error and at worst a form of hypocrisy. This does not prevent the issue of citizenship from appearing, politically, as a territory on which one could carry out a battle for rights and democracy. The illusory nature of the proposal does not preclude the possibility of its happening. Liberal democracy and socialism have made much propaganda on this territory. And yet it has settled for remaining pure propaganda, since the concrete results have been very weak, not to say null. The scale of the problem of immigration, the extent of its impact on metropolitan realities, the weight of conflicts, and the urgency of the matter have prevented the best proposals from being put into practice. For instance the debate on voting rights for foreign residents, which was a litmus test for the political will to extend citizenship rights, ran all through the 1980s but ended negatively, with the approval of the Schengen Treaty. The growing reality of productive cooperation, which lies at the heart of the new social structure of production, has been kept at the periphery of the public political sphere: the apartheid regime has become normal. The city and the banlieues, the neighbourhoods and the subway stations, the recreation spaces and the schools are traversed by an invisible but extremely tenacious line that divides and isolates. The theorists of citizenship can well seem utopian when they press the notion of a universal extension of rights.

The fact is that 'white' workers fare no better than workers 'of colour' or foreign workers. The analysis of citizenship touches point zero when it persists in eliminating from scientific inquiry the productive dimensions of the problem. Hence the inability to confront the central problem: that of representation. Even if a strong political momentum were to allow access to citizenship to most of those who, while participating in production in the strong sense of the word, are excluded today, it would still be difficult to speak of citizenship, because the problem is not simply one of equality of rights but rather of equality in the exercise of these rights, equality in the exercise of representation. In a situation where the system of parties has great difficulty adapting itself to the structure of the needs, the interests and the will of metropolitan masses, any discussion of citizenship becomes illusory, precisely by virtue of the inefficacy of the mechanism of representation. As for public policies, these have largely revealed themselves incapable not only of providing a comprehensive solution to the problem of representation, but also of anticipating for the future what had been neglected in the past: the enlisting of the subjects of production as fully entitled social and political actors. The critique of the linear conceptions of public procedures, the complaint about the limits of sectoral action, the absence of any local action (all these were continually reiterated throughout the decade of socialist government in France, for instance) have never opened themselves to a constituent power that emanates from the citizens, especially from those who are in real terms excluded from the political process. The results are disastrous. Everything remains frozen in the universal movement of complexity. In the metropolis, in the cities and banlieues, the crisis shows the signs of a sick body. To the crisis of representation that results from the lacunae of citizenship, the administrative authority continues to respond with a multiplication of substitutive interventions. But what is the point?

4   The Urban Democratic Construction Site and Urban Political Entrepreneurs

The third problem raised by the crisis of urban policies is that of political participation. Obviously the problem of political participation has little meaning as long as the problems of exclusion and citizenship are not resolved, or at least until they are brought adequately into democratic discussions on urban life. However, one might ask whether participation should not be regarded not only as a result of non-exclusion and citizenship, but also as the cause and driving motor of the latter. There is an abundant literature on this topic, as well as on associational activities and citizenship movements in cities and banlieues. But this political (and not only sociological) literature remains vague and mute, as we have already indicated, in relation to everything in sociological analysis that pertains not only to the denunciation of the crisis of the metropolis but also to a real and truly constructive proposal.

In order to address the problem of participation positively, one should perhaps take a step back. One should, then, reconsider certain assumptions of our discourse. It is in social cooperation that the conditions of production take shape, together with the dynamics of value creation, the material links, and the interaction that coordinate and direct the collective human action aimed at the production of goods and at the reproduction of its conditions. Participation is then given tendentially on this basis. The (politically central) question is: How can this objectivity express itself in subjective behaviours? What are the conditions of this transformation?

It seems that a significant number of research studies address this problem and begin to clarify its various aspects. These are all studies that stress the importance of the urban construction site [*cantiere urbano*], the birth of a real function of urban entrepreneuriat [*imprenditoria urbana*], introduced into the city as a consequence of decentralisation and of the new sensibility that the convergence of different initiatives can bring about locally. From this perspective, the urban fabric is regarded immediately as an operational environment, as a rich totality of initiatives and as a potential of productive forces. The networks and the productive aggregates, the administrative units as well as those organised by private enterprise, the cultural organisations and the ethnic groups, are considered with a view to the possibility of a complex coordination, which reveals the productive force existing in the territory [*consistente nel territorio*]. This approach may seem voluntaristic but it is not, inasmuch as it assumes a perspective of cooperative interaction in which the subjects are collective and attempts to build a broader concept of entrepreneuriat, one that grows from single groups and consolidates itself into a function of public entrepreneurship.

So the two concepts of 'urban construction site' and 'political entrepreneur' need to be developed in tandem, because in the defini-tion and in the perspective of urban action they are inseparable. By developing simultaneously in theory and in experimentation, they indicate perhaps a road out of the difficulties that the analysis of the urban fabric affected by the crisis of Fordism has revealed so far, a road that is not solely utopian. It is through the 'urban construc-tion site' and 'political entrepreneurship' that the antithesis between social citizenship and political citizenship may be (at least initially) resolved. So let us take a closer look at these two concepts.

The concept of 'urban construction site' involves viewing the ter-ritory as an interface between the objective, historical fabric, with its specific density of networks and communications, and the formation of new subjectivities: a powerful interface, which cannot be reduced to the images that the network systems theorists and the state plan-ners are offering us.

The current definition of the territory, whether provided by network theory or by the unprincipled practice of planning, is the def-inition of a 'process without a subject'. The research pays attention to openings but takes no account of resistances, of the elements of consistency. While accepting the idea of a totally exploded territory, let us continue to stress the resistances and the subjective elements that articulate it. The explosion is a source of new synergies, not a *tabula rasa* of all potentialities. Explosion does not mean territory run in an invisible yet terribly efficacious manner, as a certain pseudo-Frankfurt School philosophy, which is often revived, would have it; on the contrary, it means the invention of different subjectivities, an 'untimely' updating of new communitarian events. We should not look at networks as mathematical functions but as realities, with their historical consistencies that are ontologically valorising and materi-ally immaterial. What makes territories is subjects. Certainly we are not talking about the old territories of power (which the actors have undermined through the refusal of work and defy by reinventing alternatives to the organisation of work). Certainly this not about the old territories of the Fordist city and metropolis either; it is about new territories where, beneath the surface of an innovation that is void of sense and of a restructuring that is based on connections with no visible reality except at the level of control, new subjectivities are alive and well. From our point of view, the territory is the site of an uninterrupted battle between the action of capitalist 'command' and the permanent resistance, innovative and full of consistency, of new subjective organisations.

So here is a definition of the territory as a field of the now constant emergence of new energies of cooperation, which accept the challenge of cooperation in post-Fordism, preserve from the past the density of a consolidated urban knowledge, and prepare for the future the emergence of adequate energies.

This definition of territory also gives access to the definition of the 'urban construction site'. But the latter obviously requires the affirmation of a political energy that should turn this multiple and diffuse wealth of the territory into an operational fabric. Here we propose the concept of 'political entrepreneurship'. By 'political entrepreneurship' we mean a figure of the 'entrepreneur' that is totally new vis-à-vis the classic conceptions. The function of organisation and innovation consists not so much in finding the means necessary for capital to carry out production, but more in assembling the preexisting conditions of production – both the preexisting conditions and the conditions solicited by the continuous mobility of the social. These entrepreneurs are *public actors*, in the sense that their action takes place on the terrain of the social cooperation defined by the metropolitan fabric. Secondly and above all, they are *political actors*, in the sense that their action involves all the political functions necessary for putting together pluralities and for organising the territory. If a metropolitan area is made up of the subjects who inhabit it and accumulate their productive potentials there, the productivity of this territory is obtained by an entrepreneurial function that publicly and politically aggregates these productive forces, shapes them, and renews their creativity.

It is on this basis, and only on this basis, that it is possible to construct political participation and economic democracy. Indeed no economic development is possible unless it is based on a constant maximal use of social potentialities; if these social potentials are established and take shape in the territory, if they present themselves as cooperative forces and as cooperating subjectivities within the territory, it is clear that maximum productivity can only arise from maximum participation, from maximum mobilisation – not of the labour power, but of the political subjects, not out of their subordination and their misery, but out of their intelligence and freedom. To achieve maximum economic efficiency, the political entrepreneuriat (as any other function of the entrepreneuriat) should be democratic. Political citizenship is also an important factor (at least as much as, and perhaps more than, social citizenship) in determining productivity. In order to be an effective economic synthesis, the synthesis of the 'urban construction site' and of the 'political entrepreneur' must be a democratic synthesis.

To conclude, as regards these concepts, it will perhaps be interesting to consider briefly some aspects of the French political debate
on cities in the 'new course' of the 1980s. It seems that from the
early 1980s the experimentation with new forms of intervention was
justified by a situation of emergency (urban riots) and by the observation of the crisis of institutions, as well as by a belief that the state's
intervention on the territory through the main administrative means
had been a failure – and hence by the need to entrust direct operational functions to locally elected representatives. This innovation of
the administrative paradigm offers a new method of public action,
opposed to the traditional model of vertical integration of territories
(typical both of the royal figure of sovereignty and of disciplinary
Fordist democracy) and tending rather to base the integration of
citizens and workers on a system of locally qualified relations. This
creates a complex system of democratic political experiments that
has traversed the administration, forging new types of functionaries
and a new administrative culture and inserting the work of elected
representatives into new juridical–administrative mechanisms, which
foster a political entrepreneurship that develops from the base. Ten
years on, this process of experimentation, as we pointed out above,
was not only suspended but seen as having failed. Why? The reasons
for its failure, presented at the level of central administrative evaluation, stress that, in the best of cases, the democratic experiment of the
new urban politics would have dispersed into streams of spontaneity and into the impossibility of restitching the national and organic
meshes of interaction. At worst it would have proved unsuitable for
bringing together the complex of traditional republican functions of
the republican state (schools, police, justice, etc.) and the complex
of new requirements for territorial integration: thus it would have
functioned as multiplier of disaggregation. It may be noted that these
criticisms reflect the same limitations of analysis that partly blocked
or exhausted the efficiency of the experiment: that is, the inability to
analyse the whole of social interrelations *more directly* within the fabric
of productive activity, and hence the inability to take democracy as
the radical key to what happens in the urban social environment.

5 Always Experiment Anew

The question of social and political citizenship posed by the current
crisis of research can only be addressed as a new concept and a new
social practice.

In the urban construction site we are confronted with many different problems. They range from ecological planning to prospects for the environment, from the decentralisation of industry and digital socialisation to the construction of productive networks, from the reorganisation of services to the emergence of new forms of marginalisation and poverty, from definitions of a new labour code to the recomposition of the working day, right through to the appearance of new forms of living. But in the urban construction site we are above all confronted with a new political entrepreneurship. It arises from the fact that in urban areas, in neighbourhoods, in enterprises and in schools the very many associations and initiatives (even limited in scope) that arise there constitute a living tissue. 'Policy-makers' and 'actors' are required in this area, to ensure that the lived experiences can become moments of recomposition and innovation. Hence the importance for researchers to remain *within* these processes. Being inside means that researchers not only have something to do with social demand (the state and the enterprise), but do not find themselves facing exclusively the suffering of large strata of the population or the 'dregs'. Researchers place themselves inside a deep ambiguity, where destructions and constructions, old and new productive and social realities are mixed. This ambiguity is lived and interpreted. Politically, it is at once broken and resolved. When researchers decide to recognise themselves in the urban construction site at that point they will be able to find a set of solutions and answers that are often anonymous, informal, and yet elaborated within a movement and a history (past and recent) that impose the need for a political expression. Hence the need for an always new experimentation, which should try to become internal to the process of the political entrepreneuriat, recognising and imposing a democratic nature.

But, as we said, 'the exchange and circulation of speech remain extremely difficult' between these two 'genres' of activity that are, on the one hand, research and the production of knowledges and, on the other, the experience and knowledge of the everyday – even if the word does not flow in one direction, thus feeding the attempts at reciprocal instrumentalisation and those imaginary refusals of the complexity of the real, which are embodied both by the phantasm of 'social expertise' and by the rejection of concept and analysis in the name of the lived. Certainly these two 'types' of activity do not respond to the same objectives, do not share the same temporality, and do not implement the same procedures; therefore the tension between them is unavoidable. Their separation is even one of the conditions of any possible dialogue; and another condition is their encounter in a common zone of development, where activities, skills and preoccupations that are heterogeneous by nature test, question and feed each other. This is a lively debate that presupposes, among other things, the need not to think about the 'knowledge–experience' relationship in terms of theory–practice, because the research activity must conceive of itself and present itself as practice, entailing a responsibility, and be faced with choices and deliberations that are not only conceptual; and this precisely when the experience of those who make the city – because they live and work in it – and who build and transmit its memory is the bearer of a 'knowledge in action' that needs to be put to work, just because it is often a long way from knowing itself as such. We might say that such work, which requires elaboration and dialogic questioning, is not without echoes from and relations with the epistemological debates and contests specific to the human and social sciences, on the one hand, and, on the other, those who 'work' on political cultures and on ways of thinking and acting on social life, on citizenship and on democracy.

8

Democracy versus Rent

We all know what rent [*rendita*] is, and what a rentier is. We have all looked him in the eye at least once. He's the person who rents you your flat. Maybe we envied him or maybe we hated him, but either way we think of him as someone who – at least in our case – gets money without having to work. We recall the ancien régime as the period of history in which the laws of rent flourished. These laws were praised by reactionaries such as Burke and Hegel because they saw them as laws of nature; the revolutionary disciples of Rousseau, on the other hand, the Enlightenment reformists and the founders of human rights, hated them. The English liberals and the Kantian philosophers were of the opinion that freedom could not be sustained and developed on the exploitation of inherited wealth; that a 'dignified' wealth should be built on work. As for the scientists of the 'wealth of nations' and the inventors of political economy, they were ambiguous on the matter. On the one hand they thought that capitalist wealth ought to be built *against* rent (and that in the identification of this path lay the truth of economic science); on the other hand, they did not hide from themselves (although they often hid from their readers) that the powerful construction and takeoff of capitalist development would never have been possible if not from the starting point of a violent, original appropriation. This is how it happened, historically, the appropriation of the commons, of lands and of labour, in the era of the enclosures. So this is what 'absolute rent' is: an original accumulation that is violent but necessary – nonetheless it had to be hidden because it was infamous – and enslaving, vicious, heinous in its ways of operating. . . Of course, absolute rent has survived in the ordinary everyday processes of entitlement to rent, but in a manner so subordinated to other forms of wealth production (so

the economists said, perhaps hoped, and surely suffered its misleading effects in their analysis) that eventually it became relevant only
when it was viewed as a bonus in the competition between owners (of
land, money or both). 'Relative rent' thus became one of the images
under which the surplus value produced by labour presented itself,
as it arose through the difference in productivity between the lands
cultivated and between the trading funds. Through the idea of 'relative rent', the economist was trying on the one hand to agree with the
reformists and to find some plausibility for their arguments. But at
the same time – and none too secretly – along with capitalist development it also legitimised the violence of the originary appropriation,
of primitive accumulation. Halfway down the path that leads from
the founding fathers of political economy to our own times, Keynes
railed against rent almost a century ago, hoping for the 'euthanasia of
the rentier'. Who would have thought that the start of the twenty-first
century would be marked again – yet again! – by debate over rent and
over the political effects of its operations – as well as by the ideologi-
cally reactionary exaltation of its worst abuses?

★ ★ ★

When we study democratic constituent power in the founding processes of the modern juridical structure, we cannot help seeing that it
always touches – or rather first of all engages – the ownership structures of the capitalist order (from the critical point of view, it attacks
the preexisting relationships of ownership; from the point of view of
reform or revolution, it expresses a desire for new social structures
of ownership). Given the intensity of this intention of constituent
power, it will not be surprising that, all throughout modernity, bourgeois legal science has attempted to isolate the concept of constituent
power, to pluck it away from the materiality of the social relations
in which it was born – social relations of property, in the first phase;
and, later, social relations of capitalist appropriation. Constituent
power ended where law began. Thermidor was the moment at which
constituent power realised itself, only to be negated, cancelled out.
And yet constitutional science knew that this neutralisation was in
vain. When constituent power also isolated itself formally, then the
jurist and the politician would have been forced to adopt immediately afterwards, as a foundation as well as for the orientation of their
work, the analysis of the 'material constitution' (in other words, the
study of the social relationships that, in their complexity and in their
potential antagonism, lie at the the base of the legal or 'formal' constitution). A strange story was thus taking shape. Property relations

were the problem that lay at the base of the insurgencies of con-stituent power; constituted power, on the other hand, took property relations to be sacred and not open to change. In the formalist hypoc-risy of contemporary jurisprudence, constituent power, when it was addressed, could only be read as a 'power of exception', devoid of any content except the intensity of the decision. Conversely, whenever it appeared in its materiality and resurrected the issue of property, constituent power stretched into the era of the constitution and, pre-tending in that context to be – today – an element of legal innovation and of social emancipation, it opened the possibility of democratic institutions. So here constituent power clashed with 'absolute rent', constructing itself – as a democratic function – over the longue durée of the material constitution, and here it fought from within the juridi-cal forms of 'relative rent'.

* * *

Today democracy does not have to deal only with ground rent any more – landed and real estate – and confront it; above all it has to deal with financial rent: the capital that money mobilises globally as a fundamental instrument for the governance of the mul-titudes. Financialisation is the current form of capitalist command. Obviously it is still intrinsically related to rent, and it repeats both the violent intentionality and the ambiguities and contradictions of all forms of capitalist exploitation. It would therefore be foolish to think that financial capital itself is not an antagonistic relationship: I mean, it still embodies labour power as a necessary element, simul-taneously productive of capital and antagonist. The form in which financial capital encapsulates the antagonism is defined according to entirely determined characteristics: a strong disregard for the bodily dimension in relation to labour and citizenship; and the capitalist establishment of a masked world or one of distorted needs, of a mon-strous community of exploitation (of the exploitation of the common: when labour power becomes multitude and labour becomes cogni-tive and cooperative, capital no longer exploits the individual worker; rather it exploits the totality of labour power insofar as the latter is cooperative, it expropriates the common that labour power pro-duces). *Therefore the exploitation of the common appears under the form of financial rent.*

* * *

Absolute rent or relative rent? Rent based on an act of radical appro-priation, of expropriation, or exploitation that is generalised and

articulated on the fulness of the value produced, of a common creation of value? In all probability the contemporary, postindustrial
economist will answer my question unproblematically, telling us that
we live in a world of relative rent. But then, when profit itself appears
as rent (because on the global market it is immediately translated into
this form of existence of capital), financial rent and financial flows – I
mean, the world of rent – appear as instantly traversed and conditioned by the struggles of the multitude. And yet, when the world of
relative rent is put before us once again here, what a huge *difference* we
see in that selfsame relative rent! It – again, I mean the world of rent
– appears to be in confrontation with the common, emerges within
the common, within a generality of exploitation. There are countries
(for example China) where these processes manifest themselves in
such a 'pure' manner that social relations between the political centralisation of command and the dimensions of welfare, of social wage,
and generally of wealth distribution show themselves immediately
as a relation of struggle: the wage, too, has reached the generality
of financial rent. Looking at countries where the complex articulation of rent and profit is given in 'impure' form, such as the United
States and Europe (or, even better, all the countries of the former
third world, where 'oligarchs' of rent are still in existence), here again
we should observe how intense the struggle is for the reappropriation of rent in the formation of relations of reproduction in society.
Everywhere, then, resistance against rent is very strong. Everywhere,
on the other hand, the defence of rent reaches the point of repropos-
ing that synthesis between absolute rent and state of exception that
we identified in its genealogy. So it is here that rent reappears, placing
itself violently against processes of democracy. This is the moment in
which absolute rent asserts itself, overturning the historical course of
capitalist development as a guarantee of profit.

  Is it possible, in situations where rent has absorbed or otherwise
integrated the dynamics of profit, to define a struggle over the 'relative wage'? Which means, is it possible to define *dispositifs* of struggle
within and against rent? What does it mean to have a struggle over
income? What is a 'wages of rent'? Any answer to these questions
must first and foremost reintroduce a subject. Between which parties
does the struggle occur when rent mystifies the common of social
production? A subject, as I said: a force that is antagonistic and
multitudinarian, that has the capacity to demolish the rigidity of the
biopower exercised in the name of absolute rent. But how is this
subject to be built? It can be built only by imposing a terrain of struggle that is based on, structured on, and oriented towards rent. But

how can this be done? It can succeed only through the construction of a subject in struggle. *Rent is transformed from absolute into relative rent when it is subjected to the democracy of struggles.* So struggles will have to be conducted that can lead to the construction of this subject. The precarious and the excluded will have to be unified, material labour and intellectual labour will have to be reconnected – the former in the complexity of its factory and metropolitan articulations, the latter in the same space and in the complexity of its articulations (from call centres to universities; from industrial services to communications services; from research centres to social services, health and education). This is the multitude that can build a political entity that should enter actively onto the terrain of rent commanded by finance and should be able to introduce a struggle around income (one with the same potential [*potenza*] that the wage struggle held for workers in the Fordist factories). This is the dimension along which a 'wage of rent' [*un 'salario della rendita'*] takes shape.

Bear in mind, though, that this is by no means to think that the amounts of wages snatched from rent (first absolute, then relative) could somehow bring about a crisis of capitalist command. The struggle around income (around 'citizen income' in this instance) is above all a means – a means for constructing a political subject, of a political force. A means without an end? Yes, because its purpose is not – nor can it already be – the conquest of power, or even a long-term transformation of the mechanisms of reproduction of capitalist society. The only thing that can be constructed in the struggle is the reality and the recognition of a force that knows how to move effectively on the terrain of income. Only by taking this step as a starting point, through this constitutive use of the struggle for the definition and recognition of a political subject – only by working our own way from this transition will it become possible to open a struggle not limited to negotiating citizen income [*salario di cittadinanza*] but rather aimed at the reappropriation of the common and its democratic management.

★ ★ ★

There is no class struggle without a place in which it could develop. Today this place is the territory of the metropolis. Once it was the factory; and it is still the factory today, but to say 'factory' today is to say something different from what it meant in the old days. Today's factory is the metropolis – with its production relations, its research sectors, its sites of direct production and flows of circulation–communication, its trains and transportations, its separations and borders, its crises of production and circulation, its different forms of employment, and so on. The metropolis is a very modern factory, such as only the prevalence of cognitive work in the processes of value creation can bring about; and yet it is a very old factory, in which immigrants and women, the precarious and the excluded are equally put to work, like slaves, and exploitation pervades every aspect and every moment of life. The metropolis is a preindustrial factory that plays on differences in culture and status with various degrees of exploitation – gender and race differences as well as class differences; and yet it is a postindustrial factory where these differences constitute the common of the metropolitan encounter, of a continuous and creative cross-breeding, of a crossing of cultures and lives. This is a common that can be recognised and elucidated in the metropolis. Rent plays the role of this common: it builds it from the top floors of its skyscrapers, it dominates it in the stock markets, it unravels it to those who hide it from its producers. By contrast, an absolute democracy of struggles for transparency, for *glasnost*, can show us a way to emancipate the common. It's about attacking all the flows of revenue, from that obtained from real estate (*through* the financial articulations of profit) through to earnings from copyrights and digital productions. The struggles I have indicated here with the bracketed word – that 'through' – is today the heart of capital. Democracy can and must destroy absolute rent in order to reach the potentiality and the intensity that is required to develop the struggle against relative rent. Absolute rent, after having been the initial and violent symbol of the growth of capitalism, is now a symbol of capitalist exploitation that lives at the highest level of development: it is the symbol of the *exploitation of the common*. To stir the contradictions in the relationship between command and the common until they explode, this is the path one needs to take, in full knowledge that no dialectic is left that could resolve this problem. Only democracy can do that, when it becomes absolute; in other words when the recognition operates in it that each person is necessary to the next because each person is equal in the common.

9

Presentation of Rem Koolhaas' 'Junkspace'

Needless to say, for me 'Bigness' is the key text in this collection. 'The Generic City' and 'Junkspace' are texts complementary to it, partly coherent, partly paradoxical. I agree with 'Bigness'. Indeed, I would go even further and say that, for me, 'Bigness' is – together with 'Delirious New York' – a fundamental text for a reading and critique of architecture today.

> Bigness is where architecture becomes both most and least architectural: most because of the enormity of the object; least through the loss of autonomy – it becomes an instrument of other forces, it depends. Bigness is impersonal: the architect is no longer condemned to stardom.*

> Bigness no longer needs the city: it competes with the city; it represents the city; it pre-empts the city; or, better still, it is the city. If urbanism generates potential and architecture exploits it, Bigness enlists the generosity of urbanism against the meanness of architecture. Bigness = urbanism vs architecture.†

With this we have gone beyond the poetry and the history of the city. Between the nineteenth and the twentieth centuries, between Simmel and Weber, between Burckhardt and Braudel, the city had become a polis again and had become an imperial centre. Today

---

* Translator's note: Rem Koolhaas, 'Bigness, or the Problem of Large', in Rem Koolhaas/OMA and Bruce Mau, *S,M,L,XL*, Taschen: Cologne, 1997, p. 513. Published in Italian as *Junkspace*, Quodlibet: Macerata, 2006.
† Ibid., p. 515.

space and time are destroying this utopian centrality. The complexity of the world market reconfigures the form of the city: the fact that 'more than half' of the world's population now lives in cities speaks for its real centrality. What is present is Bigness, the enormity of the metropolis. But what is the metropolitan body? I said at the start that 'The Generic City' is a text complementary to 'Bigness', both illustrating and deepening its dimensions. I also said that I was only partially in agreement with this text. It has seventeen paragraphs, and I agree with one half of them. Where I agree is in the first half, in other words where the concepts of metropolitan identity, of history of the city, of public space are demolished; where these concepts are deconstructed, showing how much the city is becoming fractal, anomic, enormous, multinational, and so on. But I agree with less than half, especially in the last section, where the metropolis is shown as a machine that empties the city of reality, as a sociological field where horizontality is seen as disappearing, where every stabilisation is hypocritical and elusive – a city of empty spaces, of continuous panic and insecurity, of rages and screamings, of infrastructural parasitism, and so on. Here the postmodern – a fundamental category in Koolhaas' thinking, of which we already had a full taste in that retroactive manifesto for Manhattan that was 'Delirious New York' – is established as an irreversible category, as a way of seeing the present, but at the same time it is presented to us as perversity and corruption, and this becomes the fundamental element in the description of metropolitan space. I don't agree; and later I shall present and discuss the reasons for my disagreement. But first let us look at 'Junkspace'. Here modernisation reaches its peak – an apotheosis of modernity, no way out. A fascism without the dictatorship.

> Fascism minus dictator. From the sudden dead end where you were dropped by a monumental, granite staircase, an escalator takes you to an invisible destination, facing a provisional vista of plaster, inspired by forgettable sources. . . . [Y]ou always inhabit a sandwich . . . In this standoff between the redundant and the inevitable, a plan would actually make matters worse, drive you to instant despair.*

Here one is inside a Rabelaisian story steeped in sarcasm, and sometimes in dense irony – nevertheless one devoid of any kind of smile. The metropolis in which we live is a huge, grotesque theatre with no

---

* Translator's note: Rem Koolhaas, 'Junkspace', in Rem Koolhaas and OMA, eds, *Content*. Taschen: Cologne, 2004, pp. 166–7.

way out and effectively without hope. The architect is tired. That very urbanistics that should have fought architecture and debunked the architect no longer exists, except as non-planning of an indefinite and perverse metropolitan landscape. The debunked architect continues to exist as a layman, a bitter witness, and disenchanted accuser. For no detectable reason, there is here, however, a sudden spark, an event. It may be literature, but this text here displaces the argumentation in Rem Koolhaas. . . In fact this is the point, here in 'Junkspace', where a paradox appears; and it is very real. The more the critique of the city deepens – and hence the very horizon of the city disappears – and the more the metropolis changes into an infinite horizon, the more this Junkspace loses the mathematical and plastic appearances of traditional architecture and, by contrast, takes on an extraordinary corporeal physicality, it transfers the analysis from a De Chirico-style surrealism to the kind of hypercorporeality dreamed of by Bacon. 'Junkspace' is biopolitical. Just as the Renaissance scientist, growing up with lines and compasses, goes round the city seeking out the butchers who dissect calves and sell meat, and thus they offer him the opportunity to their anatomise bodies, so Koolhaas travels through the metropolis to find its body, to anatomise it. The first anatomy theatres always had clandestine secret exit routes – usually a sewer or a tunnel to the river – through which they could discharge the malodorous remnants of their anatomical labours. In 'Junkspace' that's where the analysis of Rem Koolhaas takes place; but it's also where the discovery of the metropolitan body begins. 'Junkspace', garbage: in there is where you live. Recently Agamben, speaking of the metropolis and citing Foucault, noted that the latter, in defining the transition from the territorial power of the ancien régime to modern biopower, put forward two disciplinary models: that of treating leprosy and that of containing plague. The paradigm of leprosy is one of exclusion: it involves putting the lepers outside the city, of creating a marked division between the outside and the inside. The plague on the other hand gives rise to a completely different paradigm: the infected cannot be excluded, so the problem is how to subdivide, monitor and control every neighbourhood, every street, every house, and make records of everything. According to Foucault – as Agamben explains – the political power of modernity derives from the convergence and overlap of these two paradigms. Lepers are to be treated as plague carriers and plague carriers as lepers. The result is a superimposition (over binary oppositions such as inclusion–exclusion, healthy–sick, normal–abnormal) of strategies and *dispositifs* directed at subjectifying the subjects in a disciplinary manner and at controlling them.

If we apply this double paradigm to urban space, we have a first schema
for the understanding of the new metropolitan space of the West. It is
a complex schema, in which the simple devices of exclusion and vision
(as for 'leprosy') coexist with a complex articulation between spaces
and their inhabitants (as for 'plague'), in order to produce a global
governance of people and things.*

So says Agamben. And he adds to this consideration a reference to
the control of urban space in Genoa in July 2001 on the occasion of
the G8 meeting. We might also add the control of public space
around Rostock in 2007. What does this mean? It means that
Junkspace is a place of 'disjunctive inclusion' – in the same way that
is also true of the capitalist process of production. There would be no
capitalism if it did not include labour power; and it would not be
productive if it did not suck out its value. But at the same time it has
to separate itself from labour and to disjoin it within its very existence, in order to dominate it. In the productive metropolis, disjunctive
inclusion is understood as that which includes the entire population
of the metropolis – regarded as a productive space – and distributes it
therein according to mobile and flexible functions that are basically
precarious in the construction of value – in other words in the construction of wealth and in the extraction of profit. Let us subjectivise
this postmodern reality of the metropolis. When one moves from a
purely analytical consideration, from an objective and disenchanted
phenomenological reflection, to taking the biopolitical into account,
then the picture one gets, apart from being extraordinarily complex,
shows the coextensivity between the productions of subjectivity and
the metropolis: circulation of goods, information networks, continuous movements and radical nomadism of labour power, a ferocious
exploitation of these dynamics. . . But at the same time a continuous
and inexhaustible excedence, a biopolitical potentiality [*potenza*] of
the multitude, of new excedence in relation to the dominant institutions' structural capacity for control. All available energies are put to
work, the society is put to work: Junkspace equals a society of labour.
Within this exploited totality, within this injunction to labour, there
lives therefore an intransitive freedom, irreducible to the control with
which it is attempted to subject it. And, while it is true that this
freedom can turn against itself, that the function of domination is

---

* Translator's note: Giorgio Agamben, 'Metropoli' (unpublished document).
Seminar given at the UniNomade conference *Metropoli/Moltitudine*, Venice,
November 2006.

here in some respects absorbed into people's minds (and all this is called fascism), it is nevertheless within this ambivalence that routes of flight open up: suffering is often productive but it is never revolutionary; what is revolutionary is excess, excedence, potentiality [*potenza*]. Here again – looking at it from the outside – is what 'Junkspace' is: disequilibrium and rupture that multiply across the indefinite metropolitan space. . . But this is also the moment when the multiplication of borders and obstacles, the fracture lines and the walls can no longer be regarded simply as blockages set in place by power, or as swamps in which we get bogged down; rather they can be seen as interfaces that polarise relationships. The interface is a membrane that beats in alternation, under the pulse of two different worlds, of two different pulsations of life. The interface is a place of entry and exit, of conversion and of translation of languages, of transformation of what arrives and what departs. In the postmodern metropolis there is always a fracturing of pulsations and rights, a *décalage* [decoupling] that constitutes, in one, blockage and potentiality [*potenza*] of the productive forces. Perhaps here again the link between the productive forces and the relations of production dissolved in the form of biopolitics should be considered central, if one is to understand the Junkspace that lives in Bigness. Will it be possible for them to be reconstructed in revolutionary form? Two brief notes for contemporary urban planners. Alongside the postmodernism of Rem Koolhaas, there is always urban reformism too. It has always followed the transformation of the metropolis, recognising the changes in it, of course, but often mystifying it or making it utopian. This is the fullest extent of its effort: hypermodern reformism is still preoccupied to correct the metropolis from the inside. It is driven by the ideology of transparency (lightweight materials, linear figures, predominance of glass, etc.). . . The concern is to bend the complex consistency of the metropolis to an axis of reading that is at once plastic and formalist: the architecture industry reveals here its kinship with the fashion industry and the film industry. This project extends to all the sectors of architectural production; it decomposes them and recomposes them according to logics that, in reality, hide a will to disarticulate any possible antagonism of subjects and of forms of knowledge and to flood with artificial light all the spaces where exploitation and pain cannot be shown. Rationalism and functionalism have become soft, but no less effective in their work of mystification. And here is postmodern cynicism rightly opposing hypermodern reformism: it keeps a watchful eye on 'Bigness' and always a perverse look on 'Junkspace'. Postmodernism attacks history, but it is historicising; it attacks the Holy Trinity of 'income, profit and wages' as an archaeological stratification. . . And yet it knows that it is unable to destroy it – indeed, even as it inherits it, it knows that it will end up reproducing it. There is a cruelty that post-modernism exhibits in exemplary ways: it is the recognition that the human being – the citizen, the worker, the homeless – in short all are immersed in the world of the commodity, in a metropolis that exploits them. Is postmodernism also a statement of the impossibility of extracting oneself from this reality? Finally, is Bigness dominated by a sense of impotence? And does the recognition of Junkspace end up in an asthmatic conclusion that it is impossible to act? All of this lies there, before our eyes. The sciences of the city have bowed to the biopowers. Enough! This situation cannot continue, we must over-turn it. I firmly believe that the forms of life have never actually been freed from domination and that, considering them superficially, you could even say that they are increasingly subordinated to capitalist command. From this point of view, the metropolis is horrible. And I also believe that there is no longer any hope of grasping a use value beyond the circulation of exchange value or any possibility of digging out a nature, a *zoe*, beyond the heavy deadweight of power over *bios*. And yet the more the cities and the metropolises are places of pro-duction, the more they cannot help being places of resistance. To pass through a metropolis today is to pass through an immaterial factory. And, just as the Fordist factories housed both the hard reali-ties of production and the joy of the encounter, of being together, of constructing the class, so now in the metropolis the solitude and the multitude do coexist. The metropolis is constant capital in action; it is a frenetic expropriation of labour power. But it is also a place where the multitude reappropriates the intellectual capital and the common produced through labour. Consequently, the city is at once a place of exploitation and a terrain of exodus. Just as the hegemony of the worker over the factory had been built in the communist project, so the hegemony of immaterial labour and of the cognitive multitude of the metropolis can be built, in and against the project of production, in the common. If we start from this awareness, everything can begin – everything *must* begin. I really don't know what the architects can do, caught as they are in the grip of the crisis of modernity. But it seems to me that they have to decide how to interpret the relationship of inclusion–disjunction, in other words the productive relationship that extends between metropolis and multitude. Will it be possible to open the metropolis to the possibility of encounter and of construct-ing struggles? One certain thing is that there is no time left for resistance withdrawals into oneself, nor is there space for utopias. Beyond the hypocritical transparency of the hypermodern, beyond the illusion that urban spaces can be gentrified by 'creative classes' *à la* Tony Blair (here Junkspace really does become a weapon of demystification and struggle) – the thing is to liberate new forms of life and to seek new structures of community that tend towards exodus. I have to laugh when my close comrades talk to me of communal housing, of self-managed citizen gardens and vegetable gardens, of multipurpose squats, of cultural and political workshops, of enterprises of a common *Bildung* (taking them as alternatives). . . The cynical realism of the postmodern has won me over to critique. But it is precisely starting from its realism – without harbouring any more illusions about the fact that the city and the metropolis are now given over to the exercise of biopower – it is precisely starting from this awareness that I ask myself what it means to return the city to biopolitical production – in the dimensions of Bigness, in other words not of artisanal industry but of general intellect. Perhaps it is just a question of renewing discussion of communism and democracy.

Toni Negri
October 2007

10

The Capital–Labour Relation in Cognitive Capitalism

Co-authored with Carlo Vercellone

In the transition from industrial capitalism to cognitive capitalism, the capital–labour relation is marked by a radical transformation. This transformation is indissolubly related to the mode of production, to the class composition on which the valorisation of capital depends, and finally to the forms of distribution of income between wages, rent and profit. The aim of this article is to reconstruct the basic characteristics and the stakes involved in this *great transformation*. To do this, we shall proceed in three stages. First we shall recall the origin and historical meaning of the process that led to the hegemony of cognitive labour; then we shall analyse the main *stylistic elements* that make it possible to define the present transformation in the capital–labour relation. Finally, we shall show why the *increasingly central role of rent* renders obsolete the terms of the traditional antagonism founded on the opposition between company profits and wages.

From the Mass Worker to the Hegemony of Cognitive Labour

Today we witness a transformation of the capital–labour relation in a direction that is opposite – but of comparable importance – to the one described by Gramsci in the 1930s in *Americanism and Fordism*. To understand the origins and significance of this historical turning point, we have to remember how, in the postwar period, Fordist growth was the fulfilment of the logic of development of an industrial capitalism that had been founded on four main tendencies: the social polarisation of forms of knowledge [*saperi*] and the separation of intellectual labour from manual labour; the hegemony of the kinds of know-how [*conoscenze*] embedded in fixed capital and the managerial organisation of companies; the centrality of material labour, subjected to Taylorist standards for the extraction of surplus value; and the strategic role of fixed capital as the main form of ownership and of technological progress.

With the crisis of Fordism, these tendencies became problematic. The starting point of the upheaval was the conflictual dynamic through which the mass worker had destructured the foundations of the scientific organisation of work and had led to a tremendous expansion of guarantees and collective services of the welfare state, well beyond what was compatible with Fordism. The result was a weakening of the monetary constraint on the wage relation and a powerful process of collective reappropriation of the *intellectual potentialities* [potenze] *of production*.

It was through this antagonistic dynamic that the mass worker brought about the structural crisis of the Fordist model, while at the same time building – at the very heart of capital – the elements of a *common* and of an ontological transformation of labour that went beyond the logic of capital. The working class had denied itself (or at least its centrality) by constructing the symbol of the collective worker of general intellect and the subjective conditions together with the structural forms of an economy based on the driving role and dissemination of knowledge. The result was the opening of a new historical phase in the capital–labour relation, marked by a powerful return of the cognitive dimension of labour and the construction of a *diffuse intellectuality*.

Two basic points need to be stressed if we want to characterise adequately the genesis and nature of the new capitalism.

The first is that the key driver of the emergence of an economy based on knowledge resides in the power of living labour. The formation of an economy based on knowledge precedes, and is opposed to (both from the logical and from the historical point of view) the genesis of cognitive capitalism. Cognitive capitalism, in fact, is the result of a process of restructuring through which capital tries to absorb and to subject in parasitic ways the collective conditions of the production of knowledge, suffocating the potential for emancipation that is inscribed in the society of general intellect. With the concept of cognitive capitalism we designate, then, a system of accumulation in which the productive value of intellectual and immaterial labour becomes dominant and where the central axis of the valorisation of capital bears directly on the expropriation of the *common* 'by means of rent' and on the transformation of knowledge into a commodity.

The second point is that, contrary to what the theorists of the *information revolution* would have us believe, the defining element of the present transformation of labour cannot be explained through a technological determinism based on the leading role of information and communication technologies (ICTs). These theorists forget two basic facts: ICTs cannot function correctly unless there is a *living knowledge* [*un* sapere vivo] available to mobilise them, because it is *expertise* [la conoscenza] that governs the processing of information – information that would otherwise be a sterile asset, as is capital without labour. Therefore the main creative force of the ICT revolution does not originate in a dynamic driven by capital. Rather it rests on the establishment of social networks of cooperation in labour – bearers of a form of organisation that represents an alternative both to the enterprise and to the market as forms of coordination of production.

The Main Features of the New Capital–Labour Relationship

The growth in power [*potenza*] of the cognitive dimension of labour corresponds to the assertion of a new hegemony of forms of expertise [*conoscenze*] that are mobilised by labour, in relation to the forms of knowledge [*saperi*] embodied in fixed capital and in the managerial organisation of enterprises. What is more, it is *living labour* that now carries out a large number of the main functions once performed by *fixed capital*. Expertise is more and more collectively shared, and this fact radically changes both the internal organisation of companies and their relationship with the outside. In this way, as we shall see, in the new form of the capital–labour relation labour stands *within* the enterprise but at the same time organises itself increasingly *outside* of it.

In this evolution, all of the Fordist industrial conventions – regarding the wage relation, the notion of productive labour, the measure of value, the forms of ownership and the distribution of income – are profoundly altered. Let us now indicate some stylistic features [*stilemi*] that characterise the magnitude of this transformation.

1   The reversal of the relationships between living labour and dead labour and between factory and society

The first stylistic feature refers to the historical dynamics through which the capital element described as *intangible* – research and development (R&D), and especially education, training and healthcare, embodied mainly in people (what is often and wrongly called *human capital*) – has overtaken the share of material capital in the real stock of capital and has become the main factor of growth. This tendency is therefore closely tied to the factors that underpin the emergence of a diffuse intellectuality; and this explains the increasingly significant part played by the capital called intangible.

More precisely, the interpretation of this stylistic feature has at least four major implications, which are almost systematically concealed by OECD economists.

The first implication is that, contrary to an idea conveyed by the economists of the knowledge-based economy, the social conditions and the real driving sectors of an economy based on knowledge [*conoscenza*] are not found in private R&D laboratories. On the contrary, they correspond to the collective productions *of humans* and *for humans* [dell'uomo e per l'uomo], traditionally effected by the common institutions of the welfare state (health, education, public and university research, etc.). This element is systematically omitted by the economists of the OECD, just at a time when we are witnessing an extraordinary pressure for these institutions to be privatised. The explanation of this crass concealment relates to the strategic role played in cognitive capital by biopolitical control and by the commercial colonisation of the institutions of welfare. Health, education, training and culture not only represent a growing part of production, but – even more – they form *modes of life*. And that is where a central conflict opens up between neoliberal strategies of privatisation of the *common* and projects for a democratic reappropriation of the institution of welfare.

The second implication of this stylistic feature is that now labour exercises some of the essential functions traditionally performed by constant capital, both at the level of the organisation of production and as the main factor in competitiveness and in the advancement of forms of expertise. Marazzi has written well on this aspect.

The third implication is that the conditions of formation and reproduction of the labour power are now *directly productive*, and therefore the source of the 'wealth of nations' lies today increasingly in a cooperation located upstream from the walls of the enterprise. Let us also note that, in the face of this development, the canonical model of the theory of knowledge [*conoscenza*] (according to which the production of knowledge [*sapere*] would be the prerogative of an elite of the labour force and of a sector specialised in this function) loses all meaning. This sector – insofar as we can still use this term

– effectively corresponds today to *the whole society*. It follows that the very concept of productive labour should extend to the whole system of social moments (*tempi sociali*) that participate in production and in economic and social reproduction.

Finally, the so-called higher services, historically provided by the welfare state, correspond to activities in which the cognitive, communicative and affective dimension of labour is dominant and where new and original forms of labour self-management could develop, which are based on a coproduction of services that closely involves their users.

2 Cognitive division of labour, working class, and destabilisation of the canonical terms of the wage relation

The second stylistic feature regards the transition from a *Taylorist division of labour* to a *cognitive division of labour*. In this context, the efficacy of production no longer rests on the reduction of the operating time required for each task, but is based on forms of knowledge and on the polyvalence of a labour power able to maximise capacities of learning, innovation and adaptation to a dynamic of continuous change.

Let us note that, beyond the paradigmatic model of the higher services and high-tech activities of the *new economy*, the spread of activities related to the production of knowledge and to data processing involves all the economic sectors, including those with low technological intensity. The generalised progress of indicators of self-employed labour testifies to this.

Of course, this trend is not univocal. Within a single sector, certain phases in the production process can be organised according to cognitive principles, while other phases of production (especially the more standardised industrial operations) may still be based on an organisation of labour that is Taylorist or neo-Taylorist. Nevertheless, both at the qualitative and at the quantitative level (at least in the countries of the OECD), it is cognitive labour that lies at the centre of capital's process of value creation – and that has therefore the power to break with the mechanisms of capitalist production if need be.

From this point of view – and *here we have a third stylistic feature* – we have to stress how the growth of the cognitive dimension of labour brings about a double destabilisation of the canonical principles that govern the capital–labour exchange.

On the one hand, in the activities that are intensive in terms of expertise, where the product of labour takes an eminently immaterial form, we witness how one of the primary conditions of the wage contract is called into question, we mean how the workers, in exchange for a wage, give up any claim over the ownership of the product of their labour. In activities such as research or the production of software, for example, labour does not crystallise into a material product separated from the labourer: it remains embedded in the worker's brain and is therefore inseparable from the worker's person. This contributes (among other things) to explaining the pressure exerted by companies to bring about a change in and a strengthening of intellectual property rights, in order to appropriate forms of expertise and to control the mechanisms that enable their circulation.

On the other hand, the precise delimitation and synchronicity of time and place that structured the Fordist norm of the wage contract are profoundly changed today. Why? In the energy paradigm of industrial capitalism, the wage was the the price paid for acquiring a well-defined fraction of human time, which was put at the company's disposal. The employer, in the frame of this labour time, had to find the most effective ways to use that paid time, in order to wrest from the use value of the labour power the greatest possible quantity of surplus labour. Obviously this did not happen spontaneously, as capital and labour have fundamentally contradictory interests. The principles of the scientific organisation of labour, through the expropriation of the workers' expertise and the rigid prescription of the job timings and job functions, were in their time an adequate answer to this critical question.

But everything changes when labour, becoming increasingly immaterial and cognitive, can no longer be reduced to a simple consumption of energy carried out in a given time. The old dilemma of how to control labour reappears in new forms. Capital not only has become dependent on the wage workers' knowledge but has to achieve a mobilisation and an active involvement of all the forms of knowledge and lifetimes of the wage workers.

The *requirement of subjectivity* for the purpose of achieving an internalisation of the enterprise's objectives, the obligation to deliver results, the pressures from clients, together with the coercion related purely and simply to precarity are the main means found by capital in its attempt to deal with this new problem. The various forms of precarisation of work are also – and above all – a tool for capital to impose this total subordination and to benefit from it for free, without acknowledging and *without paying* the wages corresponding to this time, not integrated and not measurable in the employment contract. These trends translate into a growth of labour not measured and difficult to quantify according to traditional criteria of measurement.

This is one of the elements that should lead us to rethink globally the notion of productive labour time and that of wages in relation to the Fordist era.

It is also one of the key explanations of the finding that, in knowledge capitalism, precarity seems to stand to labour in the same relation as fragmentation stood to Taylorism in industrial capitalism.

The same logic explains why the process of deskilling of the workforce appears to have now given way to a massive phenomenon of *declassing*, which affects especially women and young graduates – namely a *devaluation* of the conditions of remuneration and employment in relation to the skills actually used in the deployment of the labour activity.

The Crisis of the Threefold Formula: Rent Economy and Privatisation of the Common

The transformations in the mode of production are closely associated with the disruption of the forms of capture of surplus value and of income distribution. In this context, two transformations in particular need to be studied.

The *first transformation* concerns the obvious disparity between the increasingly social character of production and the mechanisms of wage formation, which remain prisoners of the old Fordist regime, in which access to income depends on being in employment. This disparity has greatly contributed to the stagnation of real wages and to the precarisation of living conditions. At the same time, we witness a drastic reduction in the total amount of social benefits based on objective rights (linked to social contributions, or to citizen rights) and in the number of their recipients. The result is a shift from a *welfare* system to a *workfare state* system in which the emphasis on welfare benefits that are very low in monetary terms and subjected to strong sets of conditions stigmatises the beneficiaries and weakens the bargaining power of the workforce as a whole.

The *second development* concerns a forceful return of rent. Rent presents itself as the main instrument for *capturing surplus value* and for desocialising *the common*. The meaning and the key role of this development of rent can be understood at two main levels.

On the one hand, it functions at the level of the social organisation of production: the very criteria of the traditional distinction between rent and profit become less and less relevant. This blurring of the borders between rent and profit finds expression, among other things, in how financial power reshapes the criteria of the governance of enterprises only according to the *creation of value for the shareholder*. It is as if the movement of autonomisation of cooperation in labour were matched by a parallel movement of autonomisation of capital in the abstract, flexible and mobile form of capital as money. This is a new qualitative leap by comparison with the historical process that had led to an increasing separation between management and ownership of capital. Why? Because the era of cognitive capitalism sees not only the definitive decline of the idyllic type of the *Weberian entrepreneur* (who unifies in one person the functions of ownership and management of the enterprise); above all, this era corresponds to the irreversible crisis of the *Galbraithian technostructure*, which draws its legitimacy from its role in the programming of innovation and in the organisation of labour. These types give way to that of a management whose main expertise lies in the exercise of financial and speculative functions, while the actual functions of organisation of the production are increasingly allocated to the employee, as we have seen. This evolution can be observed both at the level of individual companies (here one could speak of *absolute rent*) and at the level of relationships between enterprises and society. In fact the competitiveness of companies depends more and more not on internal economies but on external economies, in other words on their ability to capture the production surpluses that derive from the cognitive resources of a territory. On a new historical scale, this is what Alfred Marshall characterised as *rent*, as a way of distinguishing this 'free gift' (which results from 'the general progress of the society') from the normal sources of profit. In short, capital draws free benefit from the collective knowledge of society as if it were a gift of nature, and this part of surplus value is precisely comparable to the *differential rent* enjoyed by the owners of the more fertile lands.

On the other hand, the current development of rent corresponds to its *purest* forms and functions, those that stood at the base of the genesis of capitalism through the history of enclosures. In this respect, rent presents itself as the product of a *privatisation of the common* that makes it possible, on that basis, to collect a profit generated through the creation of an artificial scarcity of resources. This is the common element that brings together, in a single logic, the rent that comes from property speculation and the financial rent that, since the early 1980s, thanks to the privatisation of money and of public debt, has played a major role in the fiscal crisis and in the dismantling of the institutions of the welfare state. A similar logic presides over the attempt to *privatise knowledge* and life forms [*il vivente*] through a policy of strengthening intellectual property rights that makes it possible to maintain artificially high prices on many goods, even though their reproduction costs are extremely low, even approaching zero. We have here another manifestation of the crisis of the law of value and of the antagonism between capital and labour in the era of general intellect.

These profound changes in the relationship between wages, rent and profit are also the pivot of a policy of segmentation of class composition and of the labour market in the direction of a configuration that is highly dualistic.

A first sector concentrates a privileged minority of the workforce, which is employed in the more profitable and often more parasitic activities of cognitive capitalism, such as corporate finance services, research activities oriented towards obtaining patents and specialised legal activities for the protection of intellectual property rights. This component of the so-called *cognitariat* (people whom you could also describe as 'functionaries of capital's rent') has its qualifications and its competences explicitly recognised. Besides, the pay packets of these workers include a growing share in the dividends of financial capital and benefit from forms of protection related to a system of pension funds and private insurance schemes. The second sector concentrates instead a workforce whose qualifications and skills are not recognised. This preponderant category of cognitive labour thus ends up suffering – as we have seen – a heavy process of *declassing*. This sector has to cover and carry out not only the most precarious jobs in the new cognitive division of labour, but also the neo-Taylorist functions of the new standardised services, related to the development of low-wage personal services. The dualism of the labour market and of income distribution reinforces in this manner, in a vicious cycle, the dismantling of the collective welfare services for the benefit of the expansion of commercial services to the people who are to be found at the base of contemporary *domesticity*.

In short, rent in its various forms (financial, real estate, cognitive, waged, etc.) occupies an increasingly strategic space in the distribution of income and in the social stratification of the population. The outcome is the disintegration of what used to be called the 'middle classes' and the creation of an 'hourglass' society characterised by extreme polarisations of wealth; unless (and this is the only reformist option that can be imagined in the short term), taking into account that the main source of value now lies in the creativity, versatility and invention power of wage workers – and not in fixed capital or in routine executive work – capital is forced to concede to labour an increasing autonomy in the organisation of production. In effect it is already doing it, but it limits this autonomy to the choice of ways to achieve objectives that are determined by others. The political problem is how to seize this power from capital and hence to propose, independently, new institutions of the *common*. A democratic reconquest of the institution of welfare, which builds on an associative dynamic and on that self-organisation of labour that is now current throughout society, seems to be, both from the point of view of norms of production and from the point of view of norms of consumption, a crucial element in the construction of a model of alternative development: a model based on the priority of production of humans by and through humans [*produzione dell'uomo per e attraverso l'uomo*]. When, in the production of general intellect, the principal fixed capital becomes the human being, then with this concept we have to understand a logic of social cooperation that is situated beyond the law of value and of that threefold formula itself. It is from this perspective that we understand the struggle for the establishment of a *guaranteed social income* – unconditional and conceived of as a primary income – that is, not conceived of as redistribution (like an RMI [*revenu minimum d'insertion*]), but as an affirmation of the increasingly collective character of the production of value and wealth. This would make it possible to recompose and strengthen the bargaining power of the whole labour power by subtracting from capital a part of the value captured by rent. At the same time, the weakening of the monetary constraint imposed by the wage relation would favour the development of forms of labour emancipated from the logic of commercialism and of subordinated labour.

11

Inventing the Common of Humanity

Co-authored with Judith Revel

We start from an observation that is very simple, because sometimes it is easier to start thinking from the end and work backwards: today we live in a world where producing has become a common act. Some of us still have in our heads whole blocks of Foucauldian analyses on the twofold constraint that industrialisation imposed on the bodies and the heads of humans, from the end of the eighteenth century on. On the one hand, individuation, separation, desubjectivation, the taming of every individual – reduced to being a unit of production in the form of a monad, with no doors or windows, completely disarticulated and rearticulated in line with the requirements of industrial output and profit maximisation; on the other hand, the construction of these productive monads into series, their massification, their constitution into undifferentiated populations, their interchangeability, because grey always equals grey and one trained body is as good as another. Individuation and serialisation – here are the blessed pincers of industrial capitalism, the marvel of a political rationality that does not hesitate to redouble its procedures of control and management, to bite on the flesh of that individual whom it is forming in its own image and to frame those populations that it invents for itself, to ensure once and for all its power over life and to exploit its potentiality [*potenza*]. Hearing this, some people will turn to rereading *Discipline and Punish*.

Others, more simply, have in their head the rhythm of the assembly line, the broken arms, the feeling of no longer existing, the sense that your body transforms itself into cannon fodder for assembly-line production – the endless repetition, the isolation, the fatigue. The impression that all have been swallowed at once by a whale, alone, in the black, in the darkness, and are being chewed up together with many others.

All this was true. All this is still the case. However, it is the case to a gradually diminishing degree. Since it was born, *multitudes* has attempted to state this mutation, to describe its reality – this 'tendency' that was running through the existent, and digging out its inner consistency from within – to analyse its consequences. This transformation has affected, at once, the conditions of exploitation, the relations of power, the paradigm of labour, and the production of value. This change has also affected the possibilities of resistance. Because, paradoxically, this change has *also* reopened and multiplied the possibilities of resistance.

One of the most difficult and most polemical points for those who are still loyal to the old model of series production, to the symbol of the factory and to the history of working-class resistance, is to think that a new mode of exploitation of humanity – more advanced, more effective, more extensive – can be matched by an increased possibility of conflict and sabotage, of rebellion and freedom. For us, to say that the model of production (and hence of exploitation) has changed, to say that we must stop thinking of the factory as the only matrix of production and proletarian conflict, is also to say that there is resistance. When we speak of a 'new capitalism', of cognitive capitalism, immaterial labour, social cooperation, circulation of knowledge and collective intelligence, we are trying to describe simultaneously the new reality of the capitalist plundering of life, its investment not only of the factory but of the whole of society – but *also* the generalisation of the space of struggle, the transformation of the place of resistance, and the shape of the metropolis as a place of production that has become today the space of possible resistances. We say that today capitalism can no longer afford to desubjectivate people – individualise them, serialise them – grind their flesh to make double-headed golems out of them (the 'individual' as a unit of production, the 'population' as an object of massified management). Capitalism can no longer afford this because what produces value nowadays is the common production of subjectivity. When we say that the production has become 'common', we do not mean to deny that there are still factories, massacred bodies and assembly lines. We are only saying that the very principle of production, its centre of gravity, has shifted; that creating value today means creating networks of subjectivities and capturing, diverting and appropriating what they make of that common that they bring to life. Capitalism today needs subjectivities. It depends on them. So, paradoxically, it finds itself chained to that which threatens its existence – because the resistance, the affirmation of an intransitive freedom of humankind, means precisely to assert the potentiality [*potenza*] of subjective invention, its singular multiplicity, its ability to produce the common starting from differences. From cannon fodder of production, which is what they were, bodies and brains have changed into weapons against capitalism. Without the common, capitalism can no longer exist. With the common, the possibilities of conflict, resistance and appropriation are infinitely increased: terrific paradox of an era that has finally managed to rid itself of the trimmings of modernity.

From the point of view of what can be called the 'technical composition' of labour, production has therefore become common [*è divenuta comune*]. From the point of view of its 'political composition', to this common production there should then correspond new juridical–political categories, capable of organising this 'common', of expressing its centrality, of describing its new institutions and its internal functioning. Now these new categories do not exist; they are missing. The fact that the new needs of the common are concealed, that people continue, paradoxically, to think in obsolete terms – as if the place of production were still the factory, as if the bodies were still in chains, as if they had no choice between being alone (individuals, citizens, productive monads, cell numbers in a prison or workers on the line, solitary Pinocchios in the belly of the whale) and being massified (population, people, nation, workforce, race, cannon fodder for their country, a digestive aid in the belly of the whale) – the fact, in short, that people continue to act as if nothing has happened, as if nothing has changed. . . this is where we find the most perverse capacity of mystification that power has. We must open the belly of the whale; we must defeat Moby Dick.

This mystification rests in particular on the quasi-permanent reproposition of two terms, which are deceptive but at the same time correspond to two ways of appropriating the common of humanity to oneself. The first of these ways is the recourse to the category of 'private'; the second is the recourse to the category of 'public'. In the first case, property (according to Rousseau: 'And the first person who said "this is mine". . .')* is an appropriation of the common by one single individual, which means also an expropriation of all the

---

* Translator's note: Elliptic allusion to the opening sentence of the second part of Jean-Jacques Rousseau's 1754 *Discourse on the Origin of the Inequality of Mankind*: 'The first person who, having enclosed a plot of land, took it into his head to say "This is mine" and found people simple enough to believe him was the real founder of civil society.' (Quotation here at p. 44 in the 1992 Hackett Publishing edition, Indianapolis, slightly modified.)

others. Today private property consists precisely in denying people their common right over that which only their cooperation is capable of producing. The second category, by contrast, is the 'public'. Then good old Rousseau, who was so hard on private property when, correctly, he saw it as the source of all human corruption and suffering, falls immediately into the trap. The problem of the social contract and the problem of modern democracy: since private property generates inequality, how can one invent a political system where everything, by virtue of belonging to everyone, belongs to no one? The trap closes on Jean-Jacques – and on all of us at the same time. Here, then, is what the public is: what belongs to everyone but to no one, in other words what belongs to the state. And since the state should be us, then something had to be invented to soften its appropriation of the common: for example, making us believe that it represents us and that, if the state arrogates to itself rights over what we produce, this would be because the 'we' that we are is not the one that we produce *in common*, the one that we invent and organise *as common*, but the one that allows us to exist. The common, the state tells us, does not belong to us because we do not really create it: the common, they say, is our soil, our foundation, what we have under our feet: it is our *nature*, our *identity*. And if this common does not really belong to us – *to be* is not *to have* – the state's laying hands on the common is not called appropriation but (economic) management and (political) delegation and representation. QED [*quod erat demonstrandum*]: implacable beauty of public pragmatism.

Nature and identity are mystifications in the modern paradigm of power. To reclaim our common, we first need to produce a drastic critique of that paradigm. We *are* not nothing, and we do not want *to be* nothing. 'We' is not a position or an essence, a 'thing' of which it is easy to declare that it is public. Our common is not our foundation, it is our production, our inventiveness continuously reinitiated. 'We' is the name of a horizon, the name of a becoming. The common lies always ahead of us, it's an act of moving forward. We are this common: making, producing, participating, moving, dividing, circulating, enriching, inventing, launching.

And yet, for nearly three centuries, we have thought of democracy as the administration of the public thing [*cosa pubblica* = Lat. *res publica*], in other words as the institution of the state's appropriation of the common. Today democracy cannot be thought of except in radically different terms: as a *common management of the common*. This management involves, in turn, a redefinition of space – cosmopolitical; and a redefinition of temporality – constituent. There is no question now of defining a form of contract that could ensure that *everything belongs to nobody by virtue of belonging to all*. No: *everything belongs to everyone by virtue of being produced by all*.

In the texts that some of us have produced for the main section of this issue of *Multitudes* (developed from research done over a number of years, and also from being aware that this work, which in earlier times was 'niche' research, is now becoming standard practice), we try to make this common visible, to propose some strategies of reappropriation of the common. The metropolis is today a generalised productive fabric: it is there that the production of the common takes place and is organised, it is there that the accumulation of the common is realised. The violent appropriation of this accumulation is still done in a private capacity or in a public capacity – and what is called 'the rent' of metropolitan space is now a major economic *enjeu* [stake], and it is on this point that the strategies of control crystallise; but we do not wish to go here into analysing the relationship between this rent and profit, or even into the question of 'productive externalities'. . . For the moment it is enough to establish the fact that private expropriation is often guaranteed and legitimated by public appropriation, and vice versa.

Taking back the common; reconquering something that is no longer a thing but a constituent process (which means also the space in which it develops: the space of the metropolis); tracing diagonals within the rectilinear space of control; opposing diagonals to diagrams, interstices to *quadrillages* [grids], movements to positions, becomings to identities, endless cultural multiplicities to simple natures, artefacts to claims of originality. . . In a fine book, several years ago, Jean Starobinski spoke of the age of the Enlightenment as a time that had seen 'the invention of liberty'. If modern democracy has been the invention of liberty, then radical democracy today wants to be an invention of the common.

12
The Commune of Social Cooperation

Interview with Federico Tomasello on Questions Regarding the Metropolis

QUESTION   Several years ago some of your writings on the theme that makes the subject of this interview were collected in a book whose title, *Dalla fabbrica alla metropoli* [*From Factory to Metropolis*], refers to the idea that the metropolis is to the multitude as the factory was once to the working class. Today I would like us to talk about what the changes, the movements, and the global crisis of recent years can tell us for an analysis of the *metropolis* understood as an analytical grid through which we might reread and interpret many categories for reading the present. Recently – especially in your article 'For the Construction of Multitudinous Coalitions in Europe' – you mentioned the need to submit to critical testing some of the established categories of the post-workerist experience. I would like to ask you, to begin with, whether you think that this schema of reading the relationship between metropolis and multitude needs in turn to be tested and updated.

ANSWER   Today we find ourselves in a completely open situation as regards the metropolis. This is why I think that the discourse should indeed be tested; but in any case I would continue to stress the factory–metropolis relation, only without interpreting it in a linear fashion. Obviously the metropolis is something radically different from the factory, it is a place of production that needs to be analysed in all its specificity; but it is equally true that it is the place of production par excellence. Second, are all the inhabitants of the city, the urban, metropolitan multitude, to be considered like the working class in the factory? Here, too, the discussion obviously needs to be broadened, simplified, stripped of the initial categories; but *it is not a metaphor* to say that the metropolis is today for the multitude what the factory once was for the working class.

One needs to stress this: it is not a metaphor, because a relation-ship does exist, *it is happening*, even if it is no longer one simply of exploitation, as was the case with the factory relationship. I am very alarmed by those sociologies today that – masquerad-ing behind the fetish of 'spatiality' – read the city exclusively in terms of differences and separations, whereas in fact behind this diversity there is a mechanism of exploitation that operates in a manner that is entirely concrete and called *extractive mechanism*. If we take the route factory–metropolis, class–multitude, we find our-selves in a non-metaphorical situation that needs nevertheless to be interpreted through new categories of exploitation, particularly of the kind of exploitation that is called today extraction, extractive exploitation or, better still, *relationship of extractive domination*.

One needs to emphasise this theme of extractivism, albeit never forgetting that the sociological fabric of the metropolis is not the same as that of the factory. First, because the division of labour is not immediately functional, not disciplinary and, ultimately, not even a matter of control. Second, because we are at a different stage in the development of capitalist exploitation, one that Carlo Vercellone – speaking of the relationship between cognitive capital and cognitive labour – already calls not postindustrial any more, but decisively informatic. It's a phase that is now beginning to find its equilibrium and in which the relationship of exploitation – in its current extractive aspect – becomes very hard to define, because in this area there certainly is confusion and hybridisation between fixed capital and living labour, perhaps reappropriation of fixed capital by the subjects themselves, and a form of social cooperation emerges that should probably be seen as a *dispositif* of autonomy.

Q   You talked about the extractive mechanism and from there you mentioned the theme of cooperation, and then that of autonomy: a trajectory that brings us to the structurally ambivalent meanings of the concept of metropolis, which always refers to a double set of issues: on the one hand, to the new regimes of social control, to the mechanisms of capturing socially produced value, to the intensive expropriation of urban labour power and urban social cooperation, to rent, to property speculation, and to the proliferation of internal borders in the space of the metropolis; on the other hand there is the metropolis – and I quote from *Commonwealth* [by Michael Hardt and yourself] – as the 'inorganic body of the multitude', a territory of the production of subjectivity and of forms of life, a specific spatiality of new processes of subjectivation, or, to use your words, 'an institutional millefeuille that collects the set of passions that generate the common'.* How do you think that the reciprocal relationship between these two aspects of the concept of a metropolis should be formulated and analysed? By working to emphasise their elements of relative mutual autonomy, or by evidencing their constant interaction? In short, what are the basic coordinates for a work of inquiry into the metropolitan fabric from the point of view of the construction of the common?

A   I believe that the economy of the metropolis is fundamentally unitary. Obviously both the element of autonomy and that of extractive exploitation have to be considered in their own consistency, in the intensity of their occurrence. But you have to assume *the centrality of their mutual relationship*. And this brings us back to the assumption – which is not metaphorical – that the metropolis is to the multitude as the factory was once to the working class, because capital is always a dual concept: there are the exploiters and the exploited, those who command and those who resist. The problem then becomes one of combining an intensive definition of the subjects in play with this dimension of the relationship, which is a dimension of continuous, alternative redefinition of the subjects themselves – I define you, you define me and so on, ad infinitum. It is in this interplay that the qualities of the subjects are determined – with all the anthropological developments that will have to be drawn from them – and also the intensity of the forces in the field. We have to learn to see this relationship as a tissue, fluid but extremely strong, of waves and tidal shocks, as if they really were two large masses in collision with each other.

Obviously moving from this level, which is entirely real, to 'micro' analysis is a complex task. It is the passage from sociology – albeit a Marxist sociology, in other words a sociology that assumes not the fetishism of the object but the definition of the subject as a dynamic element – to politics as an *operative physics of the passions* that alone can take one to the 'micro' field. This is in the true spirit of Romano Alquati: it is not simply about participatory research but about the ability to define research and to make it function as an operational machine in the construction of collective passions (a bit like the method we find in Machiavelli, in Spinoza, in Marx the historian and, today, in Foucault – or, in another way, in the attempt of Deleuze and Guattari's *Mille plateaux*, although

---

* Translator's note: Michael Hardt and Antonio Negri, *Commonwealth*. Cambridge, MA: Harvard University Press, 2009, p. 249.

this suffers on the one hand from the limitations of an excessive abstraction from reality and, on the other, from those of an insufficient attention to class reality).

Q   You referred to the 'anthropological developments' to be drawn from the analysis of changes in the metropolitan fabric and in the processes of accumulation, and then you moved on to the method that makes it possible to use thinking and research as tools of intervention on the present. Now I would like to ask whether you believe that in today's metropolis it is possible to find conditions that also suggest a new anthropological dimension of the political, and, if so, from what angle you think that they might be examined.

A   The anthropological dimension, too, has to be considered from a double point of view. On one side there is the question of the 'mental form of postindustrial anthropology', as we might call it: I mean the subject's reacquisition of 'fixed capital', that mechanical part that human beings reappropriate to themselves, snatching from capital the exclusive command over it. The important element to consider here is that by now capitalist command no longer operates simply a kind of injection of technological elements into the human body but, equally importantly, has to deal with an *autonomous* capacity of reappropriation and transformation of machinic elements into structures of the human. Today when we talk of 'social passions' we have to speak of passions linked to the passive consumption of technologies, but also of active consumption – and this in the first place. This thematic has to be absolutely removed – as it had to be in the case of the industrial worker – from the moralism and the stupidity of an anthropology of the pure human being, the naked human being. The human is never pure, the worker is never naked – these figures are always clothed and dirty – but it's the way in which they dress and work that gives us their only reality; and this also applies to the definition of the horizon of needs and of poverty. It is clear that poverty today is something entirely different from what it was a century ago. When we talk about poverty today, we refer rather to the tools of communication, to the ability or otherwise of social integration at levels of cooperation; certainly we do not define poverty only in terms of food or housing.

And then, on the other side, we have to grasp in the metropolis a rich anthropological texture as a level at which the autonomy of the subjects develops completely and that is linked to tendencies, to behaviours that are general or generative, in other words common. This element of commonality (whether passive or active) is a *fundamental* given in the metropolis, and constitutes what research should grasp as a preliminary. Then there are thousands of differences between centre and periphery, thousands of levels of singularity, extremely different typologies [*figure*] that render impossible in the metropolis by now not only internal planning and programming but even the same topology. Now, that is the anthropological radical consistency that has to be reconstructed through its discontinuities: discontinuities of object and of subject. However, this does not imply discontinuity or rupture in a method (that of participatory research) that still retains a heuristic value today. For example: in my view, in the new conditions of life and production in the metropolis and given the reality of the cognitive worker, an anthropological approach should resume that method in which the industrial worker was seen as combining a capacity to resist and a general power to irradiate forms of resistance.

Q You mentioned the theme of consumption and that of poverty. Let's stay with these elements for a moment. Some people, for example when they speak about sectors of western urban space that are marked today by very high rates of youth unemployment, point to the emergence of a condition of 'superfluousness', of new forms of poverty, characterised by radical marginality vis-à-vis the processes of production, accumulation and exploitation, which have radically relocated their centres of operation. Do you believe that these perspectives provide an effective description of segments of the contemporary city?

A It is absolutely true that today capital does not succeed in identifying in univocal fashion within the metropolis – within this privileged place of its accumulation and exploitation – the subjects located at the productive level of accumulation. It does not succeed in identifying them but succeeds, despite everything, in governing them, in 'shepherding' them, in commanding them pastorally, and therefore in very general terms. But it is wrong to say that there are levels of 'total' marginalisation; it's like saying that the 'naked human' exists – and this is true for any form of social organisation, at least in the great 'capitalist centre', whose central axis stretched from Russia to the United States and then extended to the so-called BRIC countries. And we should also pay attention to the fact that development 'jumps', that this type of capitalist development proceeds by 'leaps' and that, while there are of course areas that are marginal in every respect to so-called development, this no longer happens in a linear fashion but by successive stages, and so on. (Note, for example, that the highest rates of diffusion of mobile phones are to be found today in Africa.)

In a nutshell, there is no such thing as total marginalisation, just as there are no such things as territories of total inclusion: one should combat the mythologisation of marginalisation just as much as that of inclusion through consumption. To me, the mythologisation of 'total' exclusion seems to construct a privileged polemical item – we need to destroy these alibis of collective action that are built on pity, compassion, and religious superstition. When we talk about poverty we talk about conditions that affect exploited people, in other words people subjected in some way to an extractive mechanism; and exploited people are never totally poor. To extract something there has to be a human reality that produces; not even those who are in slavery are excluded from the mechanism of production.

Q   Let us move on now to another radical point of view on the contemporary city: in his latest book *Rebel Cities*, David Harvey, referring several times to your work with Michael Hardt, examines the theme of the metropolis in both its aspects: one, rent and accumulation; two, struggles. His proposal addresses basically the possibility of resuming, reinventing and actualising Lefebvre's right to the city in order to graft it onto the social practices of commoning. Do you think that this strategy is adequate for the metropolises of our time?

A   I would tread gently here. I believe that the 'right to the city' should rather be qualified in historical terms, that should be the right to the city of people who – to take one example – lived in the *barres* of Courneuve and travelled to work in the centre of Paris or in Billancourt: the right to cross that bustling and beautiful city, coming from a banlieue that was a wretched place. To take another example: it was the right of the workers who came from the south to occupy central Turin instead of being confined to the peripheral belt. In short, the right to the city is a concept linked to the urban restructurings of the Fordist period. This was the city of Lefebvre, which did not yet contain the mechanism of production of the common that seems to me today to be the central element. Theses *à la* Harvey place too much emphasis on the metropolitan division of the proletariat, and so they propose a pessimistic and negative vision regarding the capacity of association, internal reorganisation, and insurgency – that capacity that the urban proletariat began to demonstrate in the post-Fordist city. Harvey's thinking does not yet perceive the autonomous movements and the new politics reflected in the new subjects of cognitive labour, for instance.

Q   Harvey works to show the 'urban roots' of the great capitalist crises, basically analysing the crucial role that the development of real estate markets would have played in all of them. Undoubtedly it was like this with the crash of 2008, but do you think that this line of thinking can be decisive also for investigating future developments?

A   I don't think that the problem of urban rent will remain so central; in fact I am convinced that in this area there will be a substantial capitalist retreat. Urban rent will continue to be relatively important, but not at these present levels; I think that things will develop rather towards the model of German cities, where the *mixage* in property categories is quite broad. Of course, in tourist cities such as Venice, Florence, and the like real estate will always have a huge value, as well as in places that are close to sites visited by 'major events'; but more generally the metropolis has to become a *hybrid city*. This is unavoidable in terms of the costs of maintaining the metropolis itself. The element that becomes increasingly important is the *cost of the common*. I have argued for a long time that the costs for the reproduction of the city exceed the capacity of urban rent to produce them; that rent is attacked directly by taxes, by the costs of services, which will end by being larger than the real estate incomes. The matter is not so much one of gentrification as one of normalisation of urban consumption. Accumulation now passes through the *productive use* of this machine, which works in a comprehensive manner, in a *general* manner: it produces ideas, languages, potentialities, ways of life, networks, knowledges, and above all *cooperation*. This is a huge 'combination', which costs capital a lot and offers enormous revenues – but these are related to the structure of the common, not to rent.

In short, in my view, the city of the future will be built not so much on real estate as on the *sum and integration of services*: this is the *dispositif* that qualifies a city, because it qualifies it *qua* a factory. *A factory of the multitude*: this phrase alludes not only to the fact that the multitude produces but also to the quantity of services, which are constantly expanding. If there is talk in town about setting up free broadband Internet access in cities, this is because it produces, because people use it, because they are asking for it, because it makes the city function better, because there are people who are able to appropriate it, because it represents a form of cooperation that spreads throughout the whole of the city.

Q   Let's now turn more specifically to the aspect of the metropolis as a place of production of subjectivity and insubordination. I suggest that we take a journey in stages through some of the events and experiences of the past few years. Recently you had the opportunity to travel in both Turkey and Brazil, where there have been properly metropolitan mobilisations and movements. Let's start from there. What in your opinion are the most significant elements of these experiences? What are the connections and the discontinuities between those movements and movements such as Occupy and the Indignados?

A   In Brazil the struggle begins over a typical issue of the 'right to the city' – the cost of fares on urban transportation. That's the way it starts, but then it becomes immediately a revolt against development policies that appear to reproduce the urban structure and are linked to big construction projects, big interventions in the urban structure. Especially in Rio, these policies link investments in big events such as the World Cup and the Olympics to contemporary practices of urban exclusion and of private sector 'recuperation' of those big community structures that are the *favelas*. Now, to return incidentally to a point that we raised earlier: the *favelas* are a living critique of those who think that misery and poverty can be 'total'. The fact is that the *favelas* are rather, even in poverty, major lungs of the economy, of productive behaviours and of new anthropological figures, of new languages, and of specific cultures – not only indigenous but also properly metropolitan cultures of the highest value. Then, of course, there are in them also elements of deviant communities, which sociologists of the metropolis discuss too little – except when crises explode – such as the drug market, which is really destructive of communities, especially from an ethical–political point of view.

In Brazil the struggle started like that, but then it jeopardised not only the issue of restructuring the city, but also all the symbols and bulwarks of a white metropolitan consciousness that were formed when the city liberated itself from slavery. The *favelas* are 'other cities' alive inside the metropolis. This attack on *favelas* thus became a major point on which the politicians of 'urban development' bang their heads, forgetting that the *favelas* may be 'other', but they are always 'within ' the metropolitan system of production. The leading Partido dos Trabalhadores [PT] (Workers' Party), planner of the socialist government, mistakenly took development as synonymous with industrial production in the most rigid sense of the word. The stupidity of this archaeo-industrialism was immediately exposed by the emergence of a rich and vibrant resistance. And the opposition was very strong; an opposition that was certainly not just 'ecological' in nature, just as it was not in Gezi Park, but was intent on maintaining a living communitarian space within the metropolis. This is where the anthropological mutation resides: the industrial worker identified the city with the factory and sought to escape from it, today we have instead this return to the metropolis that the discovery of *a commune of social production* represents. The metropolitan character is productive, not ecological, and this seems to be what drove both the revolt of Gezi Park and those of Rio and Sao Paulo. . .

Q . . . Would you see these as struggles *within* and *against* development?

A I would see them rather as production struggles against development, *production struggles against capitalist development*. We must begin to distinguish radically between production and development. On this the 'Manifesto for an Accelerationist Politics' – which I recently reviewed in *EuroNomade**– is an excellent and well thought out document. *We have to regain a concept of production as against the concept of capitalist development*. This certainly applies to Istanbul, where some layers of cognitive labour are completely Europeanised, identical to what you would find in Paris or Berlin; and they have reacted very strongly to the elites' inability to understand their languages (the situation is different in Ankara, where political elements related to secularism have been more important, because the fundamentalist Islamist grip of the government has weighed very heavily). We are dealing here with calls for a recognition of the productive community, which is made up of cognitive workers, those who are the source of capital's extraction of value. It is on this terrain – which is as ambiguous and ambivalent as you wish, yet very real – that a radical transformation has occurred by comparison to the reality described for example by Harvey.

And it is from this perspective that we should also look at experiments such as Occupy and the Indignados. These are obviously struggles against the crisis as it has taken shape in the West: a crisis involving the overall reorganisation of societies, for the purpose of redesigning them according to the needs of extractive capital. This is, then, a process of reorganising the metropolis and the division of labour, a process that envisages the destruction of the welfare system and the construction of new hierarchies. For this reason, from Spain to Greece – and in Italy too, for example in

---

* Translator's note: This is Chapter 15 here.

the demonstration of 19 October – the struggles over welfare have all been characterised, on the metropolitan terrain, as a kind of *metropolitan social unionism*.

Q   Here we are, then, at the movements of the Indignados and Occupy. These are movements against the crisis, born in and from the crisis, but then, somewhat surprisingly, they have organised their discourse around the call for radical democracy, making this element, rather than directly socioeconomic concerns, into their most significant and disruptive marker. . .

A   . . . I agree with you. But by referring to those movements in this way, I would not want us to stray too far from the specifically metropolitan aspect of things. It is important, isn't it, to be clear about what parts of that political transition, of that experience of the struggles should be accepted and what parts should be subjected to criticism.

The total horizontality – both during the constituent phase and in an imaginary future constitution – to which that fabric of mobilisations alludes seems to me a completely abstract model of political structure. It may well work in periods of agitation, but it is misleading when you are really attempting to build and manage a process of constitutional transformation. I prefer to think of a model of *counterpower*, or rather of diffuse counterpowers, which is a more open model, able to mediate more efficiently and effectively the modes and difficulties of a constituent process – by comparison to the horizontality that has proved to be impotent, as it ignores the territorial and spatial diversities that any political movement needs to embrace and develop instead. The Indignados produced real leaps forward when they repositioned themselves in local communities; the revolt of Gezi Park becomes important when it is rooted in actual neighbourhoods, I mean, when every neighbourhood organises an effective counterpower and when these counterpowers become capable of attacking the command structure *vertically*. Then, when one looks closely, that same new metropolitan composition is the factor that denies in practice the relevance of the model of total horizontality to the construction of durable projects today.

Q   Is the same true of the US experience?

A   With Occupy the situation is partly different. It is a complex movement, which arose from the problem of evicting people from their homes, so it arose from the issue of debt. And through the discourse on debt you move on to Wall Street. But then it produces little at that level, except the great symbolic capacity of a struggle that, insofar as it is American, is 'seen' by the whole world.

But, measured in terms of effectiveness, it was one of the weaker experiences of recent years. Indeed it was liquidated by power very harshly, on the one hand through the media hype against 'twin extremisms' – Occupy versus the Tea Party – and on the other through a clearly radical turn in the policies of the Democrats, which caused the movement's absorption into the electoral campaign that prompted [Bill de] Blasio's election as mayor [of New York]. However, one important element of Occupy remains: it emerged as a mobilisation linked to housing, against real estate rents, and thus around an element that is central to any agenda of metropolitan unionism.

Q   I think that we have touched on the most important movements and urban struggles of the last few years. Now we come to another typically metropolitan phenomenon, but one apparently rather 'spurious' from a political point of view: *rioting*. From the Los Angeles uprising of 1992 to the London riots of 2011, through the events of 2005 in the French banlieues, new collective social behaviours appear to have taken root in urban areas so much so that they represent an almost objective characteristic in them – as your friend Alain Bertho shows in his work on the 'political ethnography of the present', which points to the consistency and penetrating force of these phenomena in our time. On this question you offered in *Commonwealth* a 'genealogy of rebellion' that reaches from the long history of jacqueries to the contemporary urban riots, defined as 'exercises in freedom' moved by the sentiment of indignation, still insufficient but certainly necessary insofar as today 'jacqueries, struggles of reappropriation, and metropolitan revolts become the essential enemy of capitalist biopower'.* However, these events are sometimes 'enigmatic' because they are hard to grasp through the more traditional notions with which modern political thought has accustomed us to read social reality. Thus people are inclined to stigmatise them as radically non-political. What do you think of this idea of the 'non-political'? And how would you suggest that we read today's urban uprisings?

A   These are events that always seem to originate in the death of some young man at the hands of the police. You could say that this is the case of someone who dies symbolically, in order to represent exclusion. Hence there is a heteronomy of effects related

---

* Translator's note: Michael Hardt and Antonio Negri, *Commonwealth*. Cambridge, MA: Harvard University Press, 2009, p. 247.

to democratic order, the order of formal equality, which here explodes. These revolts are born essentially in confrontation with that archetypal political act – an unjustified killing committed by power. So it is stupid to define them as 'non-political', because these are revolts born from an insult against a fundamental right, the right to life. Would one say that the drama of Antigone is non-political? It's a political indignation that then radiates through metropolitan fabrics that are increasingly available technologically and susceptible to the diffusion of indignation and riot. These are struggles that are spread and organised through the new media of communication, in that combination of hidden and open that has always characterised jacqueries. The latter also had a very precise content: they attacked the centres where taxes were decreed; and they burned the registers with the names of the poor people who had to pay the taxes [*la gabella*]. This was their content, and it's worth noting how the bourgeois claimed that, when they talked about taxes, it was politics, but when the poor talked about it, lo and behold, then it was non-political.

Obviously, if one sees politics only in terms of the formal table of rights and their translation through parliamentary representation, then these movements can easily be defined as 'non-political'. It all depends on what you mean by politics: if you're a Marxist, politics is the ability to break the structure of the labour market and of the wage and the capitalist order that determines them. In this case it becomes difficult to exclude from politics phenomena of urban insubordination, which seem in fact to develop as proper struggles, syndicalist and political, on the social terrain of the metropolis. This is because they attack the exclusion that passes through the racial organisation of the labour market, or the practices of the wage, or the operations of low pay and stratification [*inquadramento*] of labour power–variable capital. The spontaneity of these struggles also has important political characteristics; and yet they are spontaneous only at the start, because later on the outward radiation, the expression, the repetition – these always involve elements of organisation. Whether they are able to develop afterwards into stable structures or not is a question that goes beyond the limits of our conversation.

Q   Do you think on the whole that the notion of the metropolis as a factory, of the post-Fordist metropolis, is the framework within which these social phenomena and collective behaviours might also be read?

A   Yes, I think so. I think that the concept of the productive post-

Fordist metropolis is the only framework in which these phenomena can be fully understood. In the contemporary metropolis the bio-power of capital and the biopolitics of the subjects mix together and confront each other: there are no other places where this situation is given as clearly. Revolt, in the contemporary metropolis, arises from the violations of a basic right – the right to live – and then expands, and normally it does so by concentrating on the strongest elements of oppression. And these often have to do with the racial dimension and with the exclusion and discrimination that result from it. Exclusion from consumption is one of these elements: which is why it takes the form of a *revolt of appropriation* of goods, as has happened in recent mobs where, through people's wish for consumption, the struggle against the racist establishment of exclusion also manifested a class position in the revolt of appropriation of goods. The two elements of race and class interlock precisely in the appropriative thrust for consumption. All of this is very effective in revealing the point of pain, namely the poverty, the exploitation. It amuses me when the bourgeois are scandalised by those young men who steal goods that are destined only for the bourgeoisie.

Q You have now raised the question of *race*, which has emerged as one of the main keys to understanding these metropolitan phenomena. It's a multifaceted and polysemic key, which has been used from the most diverse of perspectives – from reactionary and securitarian discourses to discourses that see the race question as an issue of postcolonial uprisings and to all those interpretations that have, for various reasons referenced the category of *recognition* . . .

A . . . Yes, of course, recognition is an important category, but we should be careful with this notion, which is probably more applicable to other strata of the 'exile from organised labour' than to this type of revolt, where the question of recognition may be enacted on the terrain of religion. The question of recognition always carries a degree of ambiguity related to that element of blockage or internalisation of protest that the bourgeoisies astutely try to inject into the multicoloured, multicultural masses of the metropolis. From my point of view, the question should rather be related to subjectivity characterised in strongly racial terms, as happened in the wake of the riots that spread from the 1990s onwards, from Los Angeles up until the recent events in London. And as is happening today in Brazil, where – and this is worth emphasising – together, the cognitive workers and the kids from the *favelas* – those kids who, after centuries of racial domination, are winning the right of self-expression – recognise each other in the struggle. And this breakup of the rigidity of a capitalist domination with racist connotations is an extraordinary event. To summarise: it is clear that the causes and characteristics of urban riots can be many and varied, but their distinctive character will be found in the answer to the question: 'What are these people rebelling against?' Now, those who are stigmatised by racism in society rebel against a given capitalist order; those excluded from the structure of a regular labour market rebel against the intensification of the weight of exploitation: in any event, these excluded are not excluded from exploitation or from accumulation. So the big problem from the political point of view is to be able to be inside these processes and to break them in the end, when they are given purely in terms of recognition (often identity-based, or producing mechanisms of separate self-reproduction) in order to recognise instead that individual diversity or the unity of command of exploitation is imposed equally on everybody.

Q   You have rightly pointed out that the origins of today's urban riots are almost always violent behaviours of the police that result in killings. This brings us to the question of the metropolis as a political spatiality of *exception*, a territory in which the state authorities sometimes suspend the law, rights, and legality, leaving only the force on which social ordering is based, and which guarantees it. How do you see this question and its relevance to our time?

A   Clearly the attempt to create states of exception is often repeated. But the fact that it is repeated already indicates that it is not a constant. The state of exception is a necessity set in place to ensure control, when control becomes precarious. That said, we must never forget that, in the relationship between rule and exception, the decisive factor is the state's regulation, the exercise of control by the sovereign power. From this perspective we must not confuse the sovereign 'exception' (dictatorship) exercised in constitutional terms with the exceptional norms enacted with the purpose of maintaining public order. All of this brings Genoa 2001 to mind, but that kind of exceptionality seems to me (fortunately) always more probable than the constitutional kind. This is to say that it seems to me very dangerous to treat the two as the same phenomenon, as is too often done – without much thinking and with some 'extremism'. The idea of exception is in my view basically linked to very high moments in the class struggle, and therefore it also depends on the intensity of the conflict – so it is not what Agamben and others say it is, in sophisticatedly metaphysical or naively anarchistic terms. One does not see why the bosses should recognise and designate their own power as exceptional at a moment when, if not everything, at least several things are going well for them. You have to go back to the class relation as a relation of war to understand when and how the state of exception can be established and transformed from a measure of public policy into a constitutional provision. The political science of the great Roman historians, of the Ciceronian statesmen, was very careful at this juncture. Tacitus takes pains to show that the state of exception is related to moments of conflictuality that are unresolvable by other means. The state of exception arises when there is a state of war (unless you want to argue that we are in a perpetual state of war – which would seem to me very strange). The violence – the violence of exception, which is different from the covert and much more effective violence that the system exerts daily – explodes when power finds it both necessary and urgent for some reason.

Q   From what you say, then, the state of exception appears to be linked to class conflict. A conflict from which, as already noted by Walter Benjamin at the beginning of the twentieth century, the institutions of the western working-class movement tried to exclude the tendency to resort to violence, letting it be only threatened, 'represented' in the forms of the strike. But Michel Wieviorka, on the contrary, investigating various phenomena of our present time, has spoken of a 'violence without conflict'. Would you see this as a category that could give a grip on our time?

A   I think rather that conflict exists. What is the crisis if not a conflict that has been carried to extremes, a conflict that grows in intensity from the first postmodern crisis in 1973? Forty years of crisis, which are perhaps coming to an end to the advantage of capital, with the establishment of a radical reorganisation of the forms of accumulation; and yet, in the face of the long-term recomposition of a 'capitalism of accumulation' – a new primitive accumulation, completely independent of any measure or relationship with the wage and variable capital – we have on our hands not so much a developed and insoluble crisis as an implacable, socially diffuse resistance, on which the 'excedent' production of the cognitive proletariat now rests. So conflict remains a permanent condition.

From this perspective, the category 'violence without conflict' strikes me as strange. It is one of those standard formulae that eliminate conflict in the name of violence and thereby sound like conceptions of the omni-exceptionalism of the state norm. Conflict is always there, even without violence. Then comes the violence. Why? Let us look at so-called 'extremist' violence. What is it? A violence whose power of movement was forced because nobody listened to it; yes, it was a force, but its voice was constitutionally inaudible. The great bugbear of the people who lived through the 1970s, greater than that of having used violence, was their not having succeeded in exerting a sufficient excedence of protest to make themselves heard, to become audible; an excedence that was objective – in struggles in factories, in social struggles, in a situation of enormous effervescence that nevertheless, instead of strengthening itself on the social terrain when it became constitutionally inaudible, found an escape route into militarism and was then suppressed militaristically. So, to summarise, conflict exists – and we need to work on it and develop an 'excedence' capable of blocking the 'state of exception'.

Q   We have moved away somewhat from our starting point, so let us end on the problematic we have reached. In *The Labour of Dionysus* you proposed a 'practical critique of violence' aimed at taking the analysis of violence out of the field of abstract speculation and anchoring it in an inquiry into its material manifestations. So let us conclude our chat with a brief reflection on the cycle of violence–fear that seems to be a fundamental characteristic of many representations of the city today.

A   One should no longer operate an overdetermination of violence as such. In the first place, punching a policeman is not the same as committing a murder, and yet today any kind of crime, of violence, is considered a crime against sovereignty. This is absurd, since it makes a homology between any act of violence and a murder: this is the mechanism of sovereignty, which flattens everything, overdetermining social conflicts. Second, *violence is always there*; it is not an element to be repressed, but rather one to be organised. Violence exists not as a natural given but as an element linked to the structure of the system – a system that exerts a violence perceived as legitimate. So the problem is not violence, it is the *legitimacy* of the violence – and any type of subversive organisation, if it has put it in these terms.

Now, what is legitimacy? It is the relationship that exists between the exercise of command and consent to the purposes in the name of which that command is exercised. When this relationship is dictated simply by the needs of capitalist development, there are very large margins within which the exercise of legitimacy does not work, or is missing or distorted. In fact a legitimacy imposed in these conditions is tantamount to violence. The reaction to a capitalist order imposed in the name of the state can only be a violent and legitimate response, inasmuch as it removes itself from a dirty violence – that of the legal order that covers the power of capital. It is not violence, it is counterviolence, it is counterpower, a counterexpression of legitimacy. I believe that all behaviours that involve resistance to an unjust order are legitimate. But who decides whether a given order is just or not? On the one hand, the conscience of each subject, which has been modified historically in the development of the capitalist social relation; on the other hand, the behaviour of the command functions that face you. The problem of defining legitimacy arises from this relationship, and from this point of view violence defines power but also its opposite – also the biopolitical power of the subjects.

So there is no objective way of guaranteeing legitimacy, also because legitimacy is, always, only a relationship and a means. For this reason we have to look critically at writers like Benjamin who, when they were hit by the violence of the Nazi regime, not knowing how to explain it, addressed it from the theological point of view, often avoiding self-criticism vis-à-vis the communist policies of the 1920s – although this was not the case with Benjamin. The idea of the irrationality of violence is fundamental to bourgeois culture, because the latter has never succeeded in exercising a democratic command that did not take the form of capitalist domination – whereas democracy could be the opposite of domination, if human rights were recognised not formally (= rules of the market) but materially (= common institutions). So there can be a heightening of consensus in a context in which violence can exist only when it is consented to, and not through mechanisms of representation but of effective participation. Do we want to move in the direction of eliminating violence? Spinoza's model of absolute democracy, for instance, is a model in which a minimum of violence will be possible, because it involves the effective consent of all, in a realm of equality about determining any given social course of action. But even in this case, since people are not always good, there is a need for effective counterpowers that should have the function to guarantee this process.

Finally, *fear* is a key element in the creation of a systemic violence. And it is the essential concept (the passion) around which the eminence of sovereignty is built. Fear is always fear of one person towards another, and is therefore the basis on which we build sovereignty as the thing that should remove the fear of *homo homini lupus* [human to human is a wolf] in an individualistic society. That all of this was hardly convincing, that it was an essential tool for only one possible civil order – the individualistic and bourgeois – is obvious. However, it is worth noting that there, in that Hobbesian framework, fear was nonetheless a constructive element that organised sovereign power through the alienation of everyone's rights. Then followed order. Now, instead, fear does not construct order but organises precarity, reproduces fear, is the great continent of every *dispositif* of our lives. And desire no longer goes from fear to security but from fear to fear, from uncertainty to uncertainty. Fear does not produce sovereignty but extends domination. It reproduces it in the sense that everyone should be afraid of the other – people can't go out in the evenings, women have to beware of rapists who are on every street corner, television shows only criminal and police things, and so on. In this sense fear is a central element in the reorganisation and maintenance of capitalist social forms and embodies probably the darkest point of the crisis of neoliberal democracy: so much so that serenity can be easily regarded today as a revolutionary attitude.

Florence, January 2014

13

The Common Lung of
the Metropolis

Interview with Federico Tomasello

QUESTION Let us resume the dialogue on the metropolis that we began with the 'The Commune of Social Cooperation' – an interview published in the April issue of *EuroNomade*. I suggest that we start from the interesting and stimulating comments made by Ugo Rossi, who raises three main criticisms of the premise of your argument on the metropolis. The first is an observation with which I imagine you must be familiar by now. He suggests that the emphasis on cognitive labour and on advanced tertiary services may lead us to miss or underestimate the variegated nature of the forms of production in contemporary capitalism . . .

ANSWER I am not denying the social diversities that coexist in the capitalist metropolis, or those related to the ways of life that are exposed to capture by extractive capital. It is obvious that all these are various and multiple. The problem, however, is not simply to establish these differences but to understand how they develop tendentially and which of them represents the prevalent tendential element. The Marxist method has always been characterised by the analysis of tendency. It seems to me that in the contemporary metropolis one can abstract – postulate as an element of tendency – precisely the advanced tertiary. All other dimensions place themselves in relation to it, not in a linear manner, but in any case they are heavily affected by it; sometimes they may resist it but they are captured by it nonetheless. For example, there is no doubt that the marketplaces coexist within the capitalist space of metropolitan accumulation, but it is equally clear that they, too, are linked more and more tightly to the new forms of calculation, to the new banking and market conditions related, say, to the new system of logistics. So here I agree with Rossi. However, I must

stress that the differences at the metropolitan level are not necessarily 'chaotic' but can be read as heading *tendentially* towards the
higher services.

Q   Could one say, then, that, given this heterogeneity in the forms of
labour – which obviously exists – one can and must seek to identify
a common tendency in the valorising mechanisms of capital, which
invests, albeit to a varying extent, the many profiles of exploitation?

A   Exactly. In my opinion, from the epistemological point of view,
we have to distinguish two perspectives: the phenomenological,
descriptive one, which observes and records, in the case of the
metropolis, a plurality of subjects and of modes of production and
extraction of value; and then the tendential point of view, which is
inductive and forward-looking, that identifies and affirms the 'will
to knowledge' [*volontà di conoscenza*] as a key element in recompos-
ing the subjects politically. I always look at things from two points
of view: descriptive on the one hand, recompositional on the other,
which means forward-looking and practical – in short, *political.*
Faced with a phenomenon, I do not ask only *how it is* but also *how
it can be transformed.* And, in order to transform something, one
has to assume that its present condition is always susceptible to
opening, to breaking and to new production.

Q   The thematic of tendency thus goes hand in hand with that of the
search for practical *dispositifs* of political initiative . . .

A   Yes, this is what in the philosophy of Foucault is called *dispositif,*
in the Kantian lexicon 'a posteriori synthesis', and in the language
of Marx 'determinate abstraction' where it combines with the recognition of the tendency.

Q   You talked about the modes of extraction of value, and thus
the notion of extractivism, which you discussed at length in 'The
Commune of Social Cooperation'. I would like you to say a little
more about this, particularly to clarify how you came to see this
problem as central.

A   The notion of extractivism, of the capitalist extraction of value
from the whole space of social life, reached me in various ways:
through Harvey, through Balibar, and through the discussions on
the mobile spatiality of capitalist exploitation and on the organisation of markets in Neilson and Mezzadra. These big theoretical
elements have become important for me insofar as, in thinking
about Marx, I have emphasised the element of cooperation as a
production of surplus, of excedence, by comparison with the strict
definition of surplus labour and surplus value. And then, on the
other hand, the study of financial phenomena includes – beyond

the financial convention, which is closed in on itself and relatively self-sufficient – a reference to value that covers everything produced in society. So, if the privileged form of productive society is metropolitan, the financial form of value capture and of accumulation of surplus value cannot be other than *extractive*. The capture of value refers to a space – the *space* of the multitude – rather than to a *place* – the place represented by the factory. And one can then address extractivity just like 'mineral extraction', in other words as extraction of *new raw materials* – or, better, as extraction and development of the exploitation of common goods.

Q   Let us now turn to the second point raised by Rossi, regarding the role of the real estate sector – namely that you would tend to underestimate it in your analysis of ongoing processes, and of tendencies.

A   Real estate is undoubtedly crucial, indeed central, and in all probability it works, or may have worked, in anticyclical terms, especially when the real estate investment passes through banking derivatives and the other frenetically speculative instruments that capital has used in the last cyclical phase of growth. But you have to be careful. It is true that in places like Brazil and Istanbul real estate investment has been a kind of capitalist gold rush; but there are also dramatic limitations. For example, in Sao Paulo or Rio, the use of helicopters for citizen transportation is more intense than anywhere else in the world, and Istanbul is forced to build more and more bridges over the Bosphorus as the only way to make the European part of the city viable in terms of transport. So it is true that the real estate sector is a 'pull' factor, but now it causes such a 'density' of the metropolitan fabric as to make [the city] sometimes impossible to travel or uninhabitable. Hence my hypothesis is that the cost of urban services will bring down the price of real estate fairly soon – unless the struggles and urban conflicts impose 'respect' for the metropolis by force and make possible a free and joyous usage of the city *independently* of the value of real estate.

Q   So the critical point would be the 'cost' of the common, of the services, of the metropolis in itself – far more than the cost of real estate. Furthermore, the latter – and also the question of gentrification – should be viewed principally from the point of view of the costs of reproduction of the metropolis. . .

A   Precisely; and this is the reason why 'metropolitan social unionism' also has to address the increase in 'metropolitan costs', because these bring down and destroy the value of real estate – they are (when rightly understood; and here the function of critical urbanistics is essential) the common expressed against the private. When, for example, residents in Sao Paulo fight for a reduction of public transport costs, they are obviously fighting to increase the 'capitalist cost' of the metropolis. This means that we are talking about processes that are extremely open, because they are always decided through struggles. *The tendency is always a tendency of struggle* to expand and deepen the relation of capital: it is, in itself, antagonistic. That's why I always have difficulties in understanding a phenomenological order raised against an order of *dispositifs*. *I do not think that realism is the reflection of what is real.*

Q   You mentioned Brazil, from where – again – you have only just returned. Do you have anything more to say on that country, in addition to what we focused on in 'The Commune of Social Cooperation', particularly in the light of events in recent days?

A   What seems to me fundamental in Brazil is the 'traction' of the struggles that invest the metropolitan fabric from the point of view of the poor: the traction force that the struggles of the poor exert over those of other minorities. It has been the struggles of the poor that triggered the explosion of those of bus drivers, teachers – all the old trade union categories that have themselves become minorities in the metropolis and are now driven by struggles of the poor. This is the central and qualitative element. The classic socialist assumption – which always sees layers of factory workers as the driving element – is dismantled here: this does not happen in the BRIC countries and, when it does, those struggles often express middle-class demands. Here instead the driving force is the struggles of the poor, not as struggles of the excluded, but as the struggles of the ones who are *the most included* in the reality of the metropolis.

Q   Can you talk a bit more about this question of 'minorities'?

A   It seem to me important to stress that, when we say that income (guaranteed income, for instance) constitutes a general and open measure and a precondition of metropolitan productivity, it is clear that one is not talking specifically about the rights of women, LGBTQ, or subaltern people as such but one considers them as residents of a city. In my view, living in a city is not in contradiction with being in it as a minority. It is not the minorities who, qua minorities, produce the common; rather the common is a product of the metropolitan multitude, which is itself an assemblage of minorities.

Q   Let us now come to the third and most interesting of the points Rossi raises about our interview: the point inherent in the relationship between the common and the right to the city, and then the suggestion that, rather than thinking in terms of 'recomposition', we should think of the city as an 'assemblage' of struggles and differences irreducible to unity.

A   It's a very interesting point, but it is based on the assumption that the concept of multitude is a *unum* [a 'one'], a unitary concept, whereas the multitude is in itself a machine of differences. I call multitude an ensemble of singularities that are engaged in production, through encounters and moments of cooperation in the city. There are moments of cooperation that constitute the common. In a society where cognitive capital is an established reality, the metropolitan condition presupposes gradations of the 'common' of a nature to produce higher combinations of the common. Capital feeds on the common and receives an advance from the growth and consolidation of social cooperation.

Now, it seems to me that the [notion of a] 'right to the city' corresponds to a much earlier stage of cooperative density in the metropolis. In my view, writers such as Merrifield and Brenner are on the mark when they argue that urbanisation and the encounter between differences are the true productive element in the metropolis and constitute its 'common lung'. Now, a point should be made here that, I think, will clear up a few misunderstandings: when I say that the metropolis is to the multitude as the factory is to the working class, I make an analogy insofar as the factory and the metropolis are concerned (both are chaotic ensembles from which production is extracted), but, *insofar as the multitude is concerned*, I make a metaphor. If the case of the multitude were also analogical, one might suspect that the multitude were treated as something potentially unitary and organic, as was the working class. But the concept of multitude was developed precisely to create a *dispositif* of 'assemblage' of singularities who operate in the sequence existences–resistances–encounters–cooperation–production of subjectivity. When we speak of a guaranteed minimum wage available in all productive sectors, or of a guaranteed income, we are talking about a starting point on the basis of which differences and encounters, cooperations and productions can be guaranteed in the metropolis.

Q   And, like the multitude, one might then say, the metropolis too has to be understood, excuse my banalisation, as a political concept before and considerably more than it is understood as a concept of 'urbanistics'. . .

A   . . . The techniques of 'urban order' can be read in different ways, but this does not change the fact that technical intervention on the city is essential from countless points of view. But the fact remains that, when you say 'metropolis', you express a concept that is biopolitical to the core – and here I am taking in spaces, temporalities, traditional textures, historical dimensions, cultural concretisations and so forth – all together. Every time I look out of my window here in Paris, in this huge, continuous metropolis that extends all across the Ile-de-France, I recognise layers of history, of struggle, of acquired rights, of civic consolidations. And today most of the population lives in metropolitan conglomerates; the metropolitan way of life is now 'without alternatives' in the fullest sense of the word. There is no *outside the metropolis* any more than there is an outside capitalism. The metropolis as a connecting element in terms of production, as determining the value-bearing *surplus* of extractive accumulation, is the central economic element. From this point of view I am still attached to the reading of metropolitan structure proposed by Koolhaas: a huge productive apparatus accompanied by an accumulation of 'detritus' – which in turn serves nonetheless to create urban production. But, if we follow a tendential method, there is no need to exaggerate the weight of the detritus and residues, of the points of drift and of failure in the connective tissue of the metropols; rather we should consider them as productive machines, as machinic differences that paradoxically place themselves at the highest level of metropolitan production. The fact that there is no longer an 'outside' to the capitalist metropolis does not negate (as Frankfurt School sociologists have done for almost a century now) that within capital there is always resistance and that the very concept of capital (especially metropolitan capital, as is most obvious) is a concept of class struggle. A classic example is the very high productive intensity of Brazilian *favelas*: this is what has created the shock of the current struggles. All metropolitan struggles need to be observed within the conflict around the relationship between collective existence, ways of life of the singularities, resistance, encounters, cooperation, and differences in the production of subjectivity *versus* domination and hierarchy of capital. All of this creates that open concept, *the common*. On this I agree with Rossi when he says that the common is *a machine of differences*. This is because *the common is the product of the multitude*.

14

The Habitat of General Intellect

A Dialogue between Antonio Negri and Federico
Tomasello on Living in the Contemporary Metropolis

*To the Spanish comrades, women and men, who have conquered
Barcelona and Madrid*

QUESTION   Let us continue the discussion on the metropolis that
we started a year ago with the interview 'The Commune of Social
Cooperation' and continued with 'The Common Lung of the
Metropolis' (both published in *EuroNomade*).* Let us return to
the fundamental theoretical *dispositif* that was our starting point,
namely your view that *the metropolis is to the multitude today what the
factory was once to the working class*, to turn it towards a new horizon
of analysis. I would ask you to expand on this analogy between the
factory and the metropolis, to address the changes that have taken
place in fixed capital and in the 'job in the workplace'. Nowadays it
is stating the obvious to say that part of the labour of general intellect takes place *inside the home*, and that home is itself becoming
somehow a workplace. How does this fit in with your perspective
on the metropolis? Is it possible to extend the analysis of links and
discontinuities between the paradigm of the factory and contemporary metropolitan reality right into the home, as a place where
the occurrence of moments of labour and production of value is
on the rise? Is it possible to trace the factory–metropolis analogy –
the extension of the mechanism of value production to the entire
metropolitan fabric – starting from the micro dimension of the
home, of the technologies of living and habitation?

ANSWER   Answering general questions of that kind always involves
approximations, but these offer a way to approach the subject.
So, to begin with, I remember visiting last year the Biennale di
Architettura curated by Rem Koolhaas, where I came across a

---

* Translator's note: Chapters 12 and 13 respectively.

programme note that was then developed in the course of the exhibition. It was a kind of dictionary of the home that told you 'where architectural elements become machines', an encyclopedia of the mechanical objects (from taps to lifts) that organise our everyday reality, fulfilling its needs. And it reminded me of that remarkable exhibition in 1969, 'Where Attitudes Become Forms' ['Dove le attitudini diventano forme'], now brought from Basel to Venice, in the Fondazione Prada, where works, imaginations, emotions turn into formal figures (signs, mounds, topographies and so on) of the highest abstraction – of the imagination and of desire. Now, the attitudes taken into account in the case of this Biennale (and generally for the issues we are discussing) are very different, but what is useful is the reference to passions and to the forms in which they are expressed. They are the attitudes of those who live in and make use of the 'habitational machine' in order to live and work, in a relationship by now coherent with the machinic abstraction of artistic production – as Boltanski and Chiapello had already proposed. Hence this is a place where the most concrete living and working become form: a new *form of value*. In fact, when you speak of the home, from the objective point of view you have to bear in mind, as a first approach, two elements: the attitudes that become forms and the architectural elements that become machines. This is even more true when we consider habitation from a subjective point of view: with the advent of the digitisation of society and computerisation of the city, it is possible to *work at home* in a situation where the architectonic elements and the networks of communication are inserted into the fabric of the house itself. And, if the city has a thousand times, a thousand different temporalities that relate to patterns of work, this is not due simply to the precariousness and mobility of the workforce but to the material penetration of communication into habitations and to the fact that people become singularised in them. *General intellect lives somewhere; it has found a home.* But it is a wretched abode. Since the crisis of 1973, the rhythms of the city are no longer those of Fordism – the three 8-hour cycles of work, leisure and rest, with transport and brothels organised in that sequence. Rather they are linked to the urban generalisation of labour cooperation and to a new management of work by the workers themselves. *The factory has moved into the home.* Analysing the shift that has taken place between the old job in the factory and a situation in which people's houses become the 'shell' of the new workplace means interrogating the forms of contemporary life – if it is true that production is now tied entirely to forms of life. This deep and intimate connection between forms of work and forms of life has enormous consequences, which affect especially the way people work, because when you are in your home and work there independently, you enact your work in the environment of an *abstract cooperation*, which is profoundly different from the physical proximity that prevailed in the factory. The bosses could exert *discipline* over that physical contiguity; on abstract cooperation they can at most exert *control*. This is because now people do not work on precise indications and serial determinations, but rather within an *environment of freedom*, a compound [*costituenza*] of living and working, a *dispositif* of autonomous projectivity, so to speak, located in and sheltered by the house itself. I mean, of course, when you manage to make your house into a shelter – and I stress this part only to bring out how difficult it is.

Q   After revisiting various segments of Foucauldian reflection, Gilles Deleuze proposed a particularly fortunate paradigm for reading the processes that cause the redistribution, along the entire sector of society, of elements that previously belonged only to specific places, moments and institutions: a paradigm that could be summarised – as you said just now – under the heading of a transition *from discipline to control*. To what extent, in your opinion, is this paradigm able to describe and define the elements we have mobilised in talking about the factory–metropolis relation and about the home's 'becoming workplace'?

A   This juxtaposition between discipline and control has been a useful and important way of viewing things. It is somewhat left behind, however, given the forms of exploitation that have by now invaded the biopolitical. The so-called functions of control anticipated the biopolitical type of labour. From this point of view, one can speak today of a 'biopolitical' control in which the accent falls on *bios*, and thus on a series of determinations that are much wider than those of pure control. Here it is very difficult to make clear-cut and definitive distinctions, because it is clear that both the *machinic instruments* with which life surrounds itself and the structures of welfare and monetary conditions are woven into one and the same process. For this reason it is difficult to reduce them directly, without mediations, to the distinction between industrial discipline and biopolitical control. That said, it should be added that, while this tendency – which developed over a period of time and is now fully enacted – reveals itself as a paradigm in the exercise of domestic activities, it appears under far more complex

– and ubiquitous – forms when post-Fordist value creation combines with the biopolitical dimension. We can observe the most explicit form of this 'special' kind of control during phases of crisis, when the worker is subjected at once to forms of precaritised work and to conditions of very low pay [*miseria salariale*], in an atmosphere of fear and insecurity. Life and survival are here brought into relation. And the home can become, from place and tool of work, a place of debt, of a more odious and deadly financial exploitation. From a space of expansion of desire and of new practices of production, the biopolitical becomes a prison and a force that destroys life. Here it might be useful to recall that the feminist militants and the feminist theoreticians who once gathered around the objective of *wages for housework* were well ahead of their time in understanding and describing this ambiguity of the biopolitical and the fact that it could become destructive. Long before the biopolitical had become the central key of social productive labour, these women had perceived, in the patriarchal structure of the working-class wage and in the slavery of domestic work (that inequitable composition of the Fordist wage and its coexistence with family life), the complexity of the control exercised by the biopolitical. So they demanded, through struggles, that the distribution of the wage be reorganised across the entire social sphere, so that women's work would be seen as essential and would need to be recognised as such: a wage and rights, designed to guarantee not only survival but also emancipation, in a society where everything was tied to profit. Were they successful? That's not the point. I use this example only to show the extent to which, in post-Fordism, in the neoliberal era, the conditions of exploitation and of biopolitical control are complex and the antagonism is deep-seated.

Q   Let's now try to expand on two key elements of your discourse on the metropolis as regards this displacement towards the inside of the home of some moments that belonged to the factory before that. The question of the *ambivalence* of contemporary metropolitan reality: Do you think that this notion can be used to inscribe, within cognitive labour's becoming domestic, a *dispositif* that could be of individualisation and exploitation on the one hand, but also of singularisation and autonomy on the other? Next, I'm thinking of the question of the *reappropriation of fixed capital* by metropolitan workers: How would you develop this idea in terms of the moments of production that take place inside the home?

A   Along this line of thinking, to talk of a *recuperation or reappropria-*

tion of fixed capital by the worker makes sense when one realises that on the one hand in the home there are technological means that allow you to programme and to participate in an ensemble, or in a flow of working cooperation, and on the other hand these technological means have been 'relocated' out of the factory, at home, and thus, to be sure, partially or wholly reappropriated by the worker. This is not simply a question of architectural structures having become machines, but also of a *machinic* structure of the home – and from this a series of consequences follow. The first concerns specifically domestic work, to which I shall return shortly; the other is the *mechanisation of the home*, which is closely connected to the first. Think of what a house used to be – I am not saying one hundred years ago, but just fifty: a home with no machines, where everything was organised by people who took care of housework. Inside a house with no mechanical equipment, women were forced to heavy and repetitive daily labour, concealed under the appearance of love and affects. But the fact remains that it was *labour*, material and immaterial, affective and enslaving: from preparing the food to the heavier tasks, all done without any kind of mechanical help – laundry, for example – and to children-rearing, of course. Today the context has changed completely: there has been a process of liberation of women, a general machinic transformation, which thus should be viewed in its positive, progressive aspect. This transition has brought about a substantial modification of space and of the family relationship: it is with reference to machinic elements that the emancipation of women begins to take shape – although obviously in a very limited manner until it becomes political discourse and intervenes in the structure of the affective element, in subjectivity. But it is clear that some material possibilities of liberation are nevertheless given in this process and pass through *a feminine reappropriation of fixed capital* in the home. Needless to say, with this I would not want to conceal or mystify the ambiguity of the capital relation that opens these kinds of spaces of liberation but at the same time subjects them to consumption. It is an ambiguity that we see operating all throughout the transition from Fordism to post-Fordism, that is intrinsic to the structure of the wage, and that, in this particular case, reveals the specific function of the home in the labour process. However, space is de-essentialised and is opened to the virtuality of a relationship that is no longer determined simply by *gender*, by the fact of being woman, of being subjected only to the wage of her husband, tied to conventional images and institutions of family slavery. Nor is it an area of freedom, but only a possibility of emancipation.

Q   The metropolis is also the place where the mechanisms of running into debt for property-related reasons take on more definite characteristics and where the struggles inherent in such territory become more and more significant as a result. I am thinking of experiences like the Plataforma de Afectados por la Hipoteca in Barcelona – an extraordinary struggle, whose profile pushed Ada Colau into the position of city mayor. Would you like to comment on these struggles against finance capital as well?

A   So now we come to the heart of the matter: the question of subjectivation in the new capital relation, a subjectivation that involves the home directly, when the latter becomes a place of work – which means a place of exploitation and of possible emancipation. There is in this instance a strong duality, which matches the double nature of the exploitation to which capital subjects *domestic* work (done in the house, by the man or the woman, within social networks) in its configuration as productive work, self-employed, exploited, alienated – and generically post-Fordist. There are two directions of *exploitation* and *alienation* that are defined here. On the one hand, there is the direct exploitation of labour carried out in this mechanised house, in this home immersed in fixed capital. On the other hand, the mechanisms for the *extraction of value*, articulated through that indebtedness that the cognitive immaterial workers are often forced to undergo – those workers who make the home their main place of activity. On the one hand, the workers and the value of their labour power are *consumed* when capital absorbs them into direct exploitation; on the other, capital *extracts* – indirectly, by financial means – the value produced through cooperative labour – social, intellectual and affective. However, to pick up the thread of our discussion, there is always the *increased autonomy of labour*, to serve (for capital) as adversary. On this basis, from this point of view, the struggle for the emancipation of labour and for liberation from work must be twofold – as it has always been and as it can be today even more forcefully, given the increased productivity and the relative autonomy of the worker: on the one hand, a specific struggle against exploitation; on the other hand, a general struggle against capitalist extractivism. The picture is – as I said earlier – complicated by the new elements of *exploitation* and *extractivity*, because they operate against a background of a *common activity of producing* – which means confluence of the production of goods with the production of subjectivities, of collective values and of productive singularities. If this is how things are, it will probably be possible to grasp how the subordinated, the exploited, workers in general understand today that (extractive) exploitation is an *exploitation of the common*, in other words of the networks of cooperation of socially productive workers. At the present, the social struggles of the new metropolitan proletariat seem to take place on this new terrain. The current struggles of the metropolitan proletariat seem to have grasped this immediately. On the one hand, there are the increasingly important battles for imposing the recognition of social labour (especially labour conducted in the home): battles against direct and indirect taxation, which affects the wage, and demands for generalised income (which implies recognition of social labour, and particularly of housework). On the other hand, there are the struggles against debt, in particular where it relates to house buying – like the struggles of Barcelona led by Ada Colau against the mortgage system, in other words against the penalties imposed on insolvent borrowers, up to the loss of the capital invested when people don't manage to pay their debt in its entirety. These have been massive struggles, conducted via direct action – a new metropolitan sentiment. This is no longer just a matter of defending people against evictions; it means exposing the 'institutional' exploiters and the class nature of the function of judges, of bailiffs, of the police employed in eviction operations, and of bankers, including those at the very top. And this struggle is conducted in a general manner, no longer tied to the defence of a specific good, but of the common. Here one can measure *the challenge of the common*, as between workers and capitalists.

Q   The idea of the metropolis also suggests a specific 'form of production of space', and at this level it intersects with discussions of *the urban*, which have become so fashionable in recent years, of the processes of colonisation of territory by urban technologies. . .

A   . . . It seems to me that these problems are usually construed the wrong way, by building theory on the mere highlighting of particular problems. But, if the problem is particular, so is the theory – almost always. So, on the one hand, in bourgeois ideology (and in the minds of the majority of architects), the city presents itself as a large-scale service, put at the disposal of speculation and real estate revenue. The metropolis – or the city in general – becomes a terrain of colonisation or of production of a spatiality that, through major works and the large-scale dimensions of urban exploitation, is hierarchically disposed and subdivided according to class modules. This operation manifests itself in the first place in the various aspects of 'gentrification': it takes place through continuous processes of deterritorialisation and hierarchisation of topoi in and of the urban space. In this way *something like* a primitive accumulation spread over these spaces takes shape through the decisive exercise of extractive violence. All of this is determined by the financial predilection for speculation in the metropolis.

However, a lot of things change if, in the second place, we view these new urban processes no longer just from the capitalist point of view but also from the point of view of the workers. I think that Henri Lefebvre sensed correctly the proposal that the workers were making to the city in the 1970s: true, his argument about a 'right to the city' was clearly an argument of the Fordist era, and hence perhaps insufficient today, but it had the advantage of showing what a close relationship existed between urban macroplanning and the microsociology of inhabited spaces; and how one could arrive from the enjoyment of the city to the enjoyment of the home, of the house, to an autonomous production of subjectivity. But it does this only to reverse such a relationship in a second move, affirming the 'joy of life' as the goal that should traverse the entire city, the metropolis. Therefore, in relation to the theories of spatial production – which capitalised the entire urban space in a radical manner – we have with Lefebvre the extremely important claim of a concept that is too often forgotten: that of a city that is above all a human collectivity, a place of encounters, of knowledge, of pleasure; always changing, of course, and also incomplete – but this recognition of the human complexity of the city was projected from the joy of the hearth, of the home, onto that of the urban whole; particularly for that huge layer of the new metropolitan proletariat (especially, but not only, immigrant) that had never enjoyed spaces mechanised in modern style and decently equipped. In this regard I should mention a magnificent book that I read recently: *L'Imaginaire de la Commune* [*The Imaginary of the Commune*] by Kristin Ross. In addition to documenting the seventy-two days of the Commune as an event whose story served to determine new knowledge and creations in art, education and literature in the following century, the book documents an extraordinary experience of reflection and continuous proliferation of revolutionary action in the life forms of its actors. Imagination and happiness lead to a 'redistribution of the sensible' (*à la* Rancière), which can be described in its abundance and creativity as a 'revolutionary luxuriation' in and of the city. I think that, when it comes to the production of urban space from the point of view of subordinated peoples, of working people in general, we should emphatically return to the idea of a *multitudinous programming*, that is, of an ability to hold together the needs of the multitude and the joys of the singularity, and organise the city in the service of their synthesis. I am also convinced that this kind of claim is asserting itself today in some way; and that the centres of power are being forced – always more and with more fragility – into ideological mystification and repressive programming against the pressure or desire of the governed to see collective and happy solutions to the problems of the city. When life and work overlap, the problem of the city–metropolis presents itself as one of *superposition between ecology and production*. And therein lies the central problem of urban spatiality: *hic Rhodus, hic salta* [Here is Rhodes; jump here].

Q   That brings us to a central discursive *dispositif* in the way in which today's invention and production of metropolitan space is narrated: the concept of the 'smart city' in its dual aspect, as an ideological formation used to describe the image of the city of the leisured classes, but also as a material vector of huge investments that, within this logic, reshape our cities as vast capitalist construction sites.

A   When people first began talking about the 'smart city', they meant a city completely traversed by systems, first cybernetic and later digital, that were expected to reorganise it more or less entirely. Behind this definition of a 'smart', intelligent, clever urban space there are two highly ideological narrative elements in play. These are old positivist assumptions, a nineteenth-century positivism, mechanistic and of the bosses, which assumes, first, that the city can be known from above and possessed intensely, in a total fashion, and, second, that all urban relations can be organised by rational or informatic–cybernetic means. This narrative is purely ideological. In fact, for what it's worth, the narrative element, this notion of the 'smart city', is commercial when it is not speculative. It is something of a con: an attempt to sell a product at a higher price than it's worth. That intelligence that – according to the adverts – runs through and encompasses everything is in reality nothing but control: control over the labour that develops in the city, necessary to social exploitation, and control through the violence necessary to ensure an ordered process. The 'smart city' and the 'smart society' are, to my mind, pure mystifications. However, they become antagonistically embroiled in a real process, which is tied to the new centrality that the communicative flows confer upon labour in the structure of the metropolis. The increase in the structural connections of communication produces a *surplus value* that is directly extracted by capital and, at the same time, a *resistance* – and thus a possibility of attacking capital, which is constrained to this high level of mystification. This resistance appears not as one act of becoming aware but rather as a *continuity of* daily *elements of rupture* – of a molecular action – related to the malaise of urban living. To get a decent life you have to shake up the metropolitan life that capital would like to reduce to the quiet of the small towns of ten thousand inhabitants of the early twentieth century, a quiet renewed by television, which replaces the parish priest in functions of spiritual guidance. In consequence, paradoxically, the 'smart city' needs urban 'hackers'. And, on the other hand, without urban hackers the possibility of resistance and encounter, which constitutes the pleasure of living in the metropolis, would never have been born.

Q   In a mirroring position from the rhetoric of the 'smart city' we find the representation of urban peripheries, favelas, slums, banlieues – with all the evocative power [*potenza*] that this last word acquires from its etymological root, which is related to the feudal institution of the 'edict' [*'bando'*].* In our previous interviews you emphasised the *productive* character of these places of common labour or resistance and the importance of the conflicts that take shape there. Would you like to add something on this theme, in view of the path we have followed today in our investigation?

A   When we talk of these peripheries it is not enough to cite the analyses, studies and opinions developed by writers such as Mike Davis, for example. These researches have focused primarily on the *alienation* of the poor in the city, considering their social dangerousness as a provocation against an increasingly thorough control and, on the other hand, as a *dispositif* for emancipation in these alienated places. But I believe that, far from alienation, those proletarian and poor places represent, powerfully, a *common quality* of urban life and metropolitan labour – something hard to erase. There are too many phenomenologies about those with no rights or the outcasts, and all of them perceive banlieues as places of total exclusion. My experience as a researcher of banlieues has always led me to avoid totalisations and has always disclosed to me, by contrast, a richness in working capacities and a quality of coexistence and cooperation, both of them often creative. These banlieues

---

* Translator's note: Old French *ban* ('proclamation', 'decree' of an overlord).

are periodically absorbed or periodically rejected by large capitalist enterprises, which invest them in terms of both the labour market and the user goods produced there – especially cultural goods, music, ways of living, and so on. Thus we witness a continuous alternation between integration and banning, between absorption and exclusion, and it is important to highlight the antagonist centrality assumed by the banlieues between accumulated misery and rebellious determination. This is not 'bare life'; the biopolitical rhythm is rather full of contradictions, sometimes antinomic (religion–integration, for example). Life, even at its core, is full of conflict and ready to explode.

Q   In the work of many writers, the theme of extractivism that you put at the heart of the discourse on the contemporary metropolis is closely related to the uninterrupted and never completed character of what Marx called 'primitive accumulation' when he described how capital 'comes dripping from head to foot, from every pore, with blood and dirt'* through processes of ruthless and bloody expropriation. Do you think that in the contemporary metropolis it is possible to describe a similar violence as being inherent to the processes of extraction of value? What is the specific violence of the contemporary metropolis in the subjective sense of the genitive†?

A   I think that the insistence – if not exclusive, then certainly prevailing – on the violence of neoliberal control has given false images of some aspects of the contemporary post-Fordist metropolis. Specifically, I believe that the oft-repeated analogy with primitive accumulation can produce major misunderstandings. It is in fact clear, on the one hand, that the singularisation of the home that we discussed is entirely specific to extractive mechanisms and to the subsumption of the metropolis in the cycle of financial capital. It is also clear, however, that there are various responses, various epistemologies, which oppose extractivism with some force. It is true that in the regime of the 'big factory' what was called 'real subsumption' – the unitary and compact imposition of the process of valorisation – is today coming apart and reopening with evident

---

* Translator's note: This comes at the end of ch. 31 in *Capital*, vol. 1.
† Translator's note: i.e. when 'the contemporary metropolis' is subject rather than object of this violence. Subjective (and objective) genitive is a grammatical category from Latin, where the genitive in expressions like *amor fratris* ('love of a brother') could turn either into subject – *frater amat* ('the brother loves [x]') – or into direct object – *fratrem amat* ('[x] loves the brother') when the expressions in question took propositional form.

spatial discontinuities and multiple temporal rhythms. However, in the metropolis of general intellect one should be very careful about speaking of a new 'primitive accumulation', or even of new episodes of 'formal subsumption', because, if these exist, they exist anyway in the metropolis of the general intellect, within the conditions imposed by this latest transition in and of the structure of capital – following on from the stages of primitive accumulation (in the proper sense), of simple cooperation, and of big industry. If there are phenomena that recall 'primitive accumulation' and 'formal subsumption', one should bear in mind that they are not phenomena that repeat what Marx described in *Capital* 150 years ago, but new processes whose ingredients have all been modified. It seems to me crucial that, while the metropolis of the general intellect is beyond doubt a reality on which capitalist violence is exercised, this violence is restrained, conditioned, matched to local realities, by the need to construct productive cooperation – which draws its tools from the labour power disseminated over the territory. Capitalist violence comes up against formidable limits in confrontation with general intellect and with the organisation of labour in the metropolis of general intellect. It is no accident that capital's control is reorganised through an exercise of violence that supplements productive and financial instruments with policing and cultural instruments: basically *a production of fear*. Multiplied in all forms that fear can take and introjected through the media, this is probably the greatest violence that is exerted on the contemporary metropolis. Fear of the other, of epidemics, of pollution, and so on – on the understanding that extractivism is not only the latest (chronologically) but also the highest form of violence – and yet one with unbalanced results, considering what capitalist violence was able to obtain in earlier stages of development. In short, this violence must not be confused with the old narratives, because, in the process that brought us to the present times, the force of the multitude, too, became increasingly restless and dangerous for capital, for the exercise of its command – and this particularly in metropolises.

Q   Many years before writing the twenty-fourth chapter of the first volume of *Capital* on primitive accumulation, a very young Marx had already become interested in the process of expropriation of the natural common [*il comune naturale*]. Writing about the laws against the thefts of wood perpetrated by peasants on lands that had once been common, he adduced the issue of usage, the customary right of the people. Do you think that the matter of usage, from the point of view of its relation to the common, might have any topicality for the contemporary metropolitan fabric, marked as it is by mechanisms of extractive accumulation?

A   I think that the social formation produces and at the same time is the product of the process of production. The common therefore accompanies extractive exploitation; it produces it and is its product. But your question takes me into a reality which I understand immediately, as a *dispositif* of struggle. And so I stipulate, I decide that the common precedes the extractivism. From this point of view, *there is no extractivism unless the common exists*. The 'real subsumption' of society to capital produces this effect, of *communalising labour*. But it is biopolitical labour, in other words a kind of labour that acquires value in proportion to how common, socialised and cooperative it is. We are in a reverse process by comparison to the one analysed by Marx in relation to primitive accumulation and the expropriation of the 'natural' common. Today the contradiction of capitalist exploitation is organised in the urgent need to expropriate the common through the public, which is commanded by the private: the public is no longer a defence or bulwark against privatisations. Now the US Supreme Court legitimises expropriation for the necessities of capitalist development. In other words, the public (the Supreme Court) legitimises the expropriation of the common (spaces, activities) so as to allow the private (a multinational, in the instance I have in mind) to develop. At one time the public was supplementary and could become a subsidiary of the private: where the private did not reach – in building infrastructures, railways, airports, schools, hospitals, and so on – it was the public that went ahead. Today these large service structures – this common that has integrated the natural common – are to be removed from the public and reprivatised. Is the common stronger? Will it succeed in defending itself? Will it be able to rebel against a command oriented towards privatising and block its development? This is today's battlefield; it's already strongly biased – but a battlefield nonetheless.

Q   Let us conclude this three-phase dialogue of ours on the metropolis with a question about whether it is possible to think of a specificity of 'metropolitan politics', a specific form of political action within these *'common' totalities*, articulated in correspondence with the contemporary forms of production of subjectivity and the common.

A   The fact that nowadays architects increasingly think of 'operating on the ground' is immediately political. There are comrades in architecture who try to translate into their work workerist options reinterpreted in social terms (for example Aureli and his group), and they tend to push architecture to place itself in an 'ancillary' or enabling position vis-à-vis the necessities of liberation – in other words the needs of the multitude and of political struggles. Up until now the ancillary character of architecture has always been as the prerogative of real estate big capitalism. Now, even at the professional level, it means rather the need, neither ingenuous nor utopian, to *build according to norms of the common*. And by this I mean the possibility of encouraging cooperation and freedom, equality and solidarity, and of rescuing the city, in its singular plurality, from the forced homogenisation that capital wants to impose on it. It is within this space and these parameters that ecological struggles, for example, turn from the defence of nature to the 'Charter of the Forests' – the defence and construction of the metropolitan common. A method that proposes alternatives to the capitalist plan has to be antagonistic here. It is on this terrain that the multitude organises itself as a physical and urban character. I believe – following the good old workerist point of view – that struggles always precede capitalist structuring: today, in the metropolis, this relationship (no longer dialectical but antagonist) becomes central. *The metropolises become a privileged terrain of class struggle, and also of social struggle. The metropolis is effectively a factory*, but *a factory of general intellect*. And the labour power of general intellect is as dynamic, mobile, flexible, and powerful as was that of the glorious working class. And probably more so.

To conclude. I began by highlighting the fact that, in today's metropolis, macro and micro are in correspondence within a functional relationship and at the same time are in a harsh confrontation. I continued by trying to see, at various levels, how the relation of domination that capital exerts in its action on the metropolis can be resisted, interrupted, turned into alternative forms; also how subordination to fixed capital can be reversed and how resistance to alienation can get the upper hand over sad passions. These considerations lead me to see in the city–metropolis not only the fundamental place in which extractive exploitation is exercised but also the possible space for a political recomposition of resistances. Thus productive cooperation – strongly accentuated by the present transformations in technology, which the city promotes and imposes – constitutes an exceptional space of exploitation; well, this accentuation of productive cooperation nevertheless opens the possibility of an antagonist organisation and a radical alternative.

Even more interesting is the analysis of the 'time of the metropolis'. More than two thirds of humanity now live in extremely massified metropolitan areas: the transformation of mankind that Machiavelli described when talking of the city, from 'beast' into 'citizen', takes place in these areas – or rather took place. Now it is necessary for citizens to discover themselves as *producers* of the place they inhabit; that they take into their hands the keys to interpreting, constructing and acting in the city. But the U-turn from the condition of exploited producers to that of creative producers is neither automatic nor spontaneous. However, it is not an impossible route either, or one too difficult to follow. It is a route that can be sustained only on a radical transformation of being common, of living in common. To pursue this route, to make it so that the path is itself revolutionary, we need to build mutualistic forms of life, unions of the social, laboratories of encounters and action. Where? How? In the metropolis, in the streets and squares. Municipalism (i.e., [the programme of] organising and struggling in the municipalities) indicates the *where*. It is a generic indication but often very helpful. As to the *how*, the history of workers' struggles shows us the way to move, translating the strike that 'hurts the boss' into a struggle that occasions hurt for the bosses of the city. Translate the factory struggle and the political struggles of old-style socialism into modes of attacking extractive capital: this is the way to a communism of tomorrow. In the city, in the metropolis. And it will not be difficult if we remember, as Kristin Ross reminds us, that Marxian insight that the revolutionary working-class movement had already adopted as a mark of its own writing of history – and now it is up to us, as citizens, to make it our own:*

> when labor time ceases to be the measure of work and work the measure of wealth, then wealth will no longer be measurable in terms of exchange value. Just as for each of these thinkers true individualism was only possible under communism, which needs and values the contribution of each individual to the common good, so true luxury could only be communal luxury.

---

* Translator's note: Kristin Ross, *Communal Luxury: The Political Imaginary of the Paris Commune*, Verso, London, 2015, p. 142.

Part III

First Fruits of the New Metropolis

15

Reflections on 'Manifesto for an Accelerationist Politics'

The 'Manifesto for an Accelerationist Politics'* begins with a broad statement of the dramatic nature of the current crisis – a cataclysm . . . – but also with a negation of the future: an impending apocalypse. No need to get alarmed – there is nothing theological–political in this; anyone looking for that kind of thing can stop reading right here. Nor will you find any of the current shibboleths – or rather it is only noted in passing: the collapse of the planet's climate system. Yes, important, but entirely an outcome of industrial policies and approachable only on the basis of criticising them. What it sees as crucial, rather, is 'the increasing automation of production processes' – including 'intellectual labour' – and this is taken as proof of the definitive crisis of capitalism. Is this catastrophism? An improper use of the categories of the falling rate of profit? I would say not. Rather the reality of the crisis is identified here with the aggression that neoliberalism has developed against the entire structure of class relations organised in the social state of the nineteenth and twentieth centuries; the cause of the crisis is identified with the blockage of productive capacities – a necessity derived from the forms of capitalist command against the new character of living labour. A harsh critique of the governing forces of the right follows – and with it a critique of much of what remains of the forces of the left – the latter often deluded (in the best of cases) by new and impossible hypotheses of Keynesian resistances and at any rate unable to imagine a radical alternative. What has been deleted from this condition is the future; what has been

---

* Translator's note: Alex Williams and Nick Srnicek, 'Accelerate: Manifesto for an Accelerationist Politics', at http://criticallegalthinking.com/2013/05/14/accelerate-manifesto-for-an-accelerationist-politics.

imposed is a real paralysis of political imaginary. Spontaneity will not be enough to take you out of this condition. Only a systematic class approach to the construction of a new economy and to a new political organisation of workers will be able to rebuild a hegemony in which proletarian hands will hold a possible future.

There is still room for a subversive knowledge!

This opening is what is required for the communist task as it presents itself today. It is a step forward, determined and decisive, for people interested in thinking about revolution. But, above all, it gives the movement a new 'form' – and by 'form' I mean that *dispositif* that is constitutive, rich in potentiality, and ready to break with the hierarchical and repressive state horizon that gives meaning to capitalist power in our days. This is not about overturning the 'state form'; it is rather a reference to *potenza* [potential] against *potere* [power], for biopolitics against biopower. It is here, in this premise where the possibility of an emancipatory future opposes radically this present of domination, that we have that 'one divided into two' that constitutes today (rather than a conclusion) the only rational premise of subversive practice.

But let us move on, to see how the theory develops. The Manifesto's hypothesis is that, within the evolution of capital, we have to liberate the potentiality of labour against the blockage that capitalism creates; we have to pursue the constant economic growth and technological development (accompanied by growing social inequalities) and to effect a complete internal overturning of the class relation. Here the notion of 'inside–against' returns – a refrain from the workerist tradition. The process of liberation can only occur by accelerating the development of capitalism, without, however, confusing acceleration with speed (and this is important), because here the acceleration has all the characteristics of a motor-*dispositif*, of an experimental process of discovery and creation within the space of possibilities brought about by capitalism itself. The Marxist concept of 'tendency' is here coupled with the spatial analysis of the parameters of development – to that insistence on 'ground' [*terra*] (territorialisation and deterritorialisation) that was characteristic of Deleuze and Guattari. And there is another fundamental element: the potentiality of cognitive labour that capitalism brings about but represses, that it constitutes but reduces within the growing algorithmic automation of domination, that it valorises ontologically (a growing production of value) but also devalues from a monetary and disciplinary point of view (not only in crisis but all throughout the story of its development, and in particular through its management of the 'state form'). So. . . this potentiality [*potenza*], with due respect to all those who still flap about, claiming that the possibility of revolution depends on the rebirth of a twentieth-century working class, makes it clear that here there is a class, but a class that is quite different, with a much higher potential [*potenza*], and it is the class of cognitive labour: this is the class that has to be liberated, this is the class that must liberate itself.

The recovery of the Marxist and Leninist concept of tendency is here complete. And this also snatches away, so to speak, any 'futurist' illusions, since it is the class struggle that determines not only the movement but also the ability to turn its highest abstraction into a solid machine of struggle.

This capacity to liberate the productive forces of cognitive labour is the basis for the whole discourse of the Manifesto. We have to rid ourselves of the illusion of a return to Fordist labour, we have to grasp definitively the transition from the hegemony of material labour to that of immaterial labour, and then, given capitalism's command over technologies, we have to attack 'capital's increasingly retrograde approach to technology'. The productive forces end up being limited by capitalist command. The key issue thus is, then, that of liberating the *latent* productive forces, just as revolutionary materialism has always done. It is this question of 'latency' that we now need to examine.

But first we have to ask ourselves why it is that, not by chance, a great deal of the Manifesto's attention turns at this point to the question of organisation. A powerful critique develops here against any concept of 'horizontal', 'spontaneous' organisation of the movements, against any conception of 'democracy as a process'. In the Manifesto's view, these are purely and simply fetishistic determinations (of democracy) that have no effectual consequence, either destructive [*destituente*] or constructive [*costituente*], as regards the capitalist institutions of command. This last claim is perhaps excessive, when we consider the current movements that do in fact set themselves forcefully (and without alternatives or appropriate tools) against finance capital and its institutional productions. But it is certain that you cannot avoid a strong institutional transition, stronger than democratic horizontality will ever be able to propose, when you speak of revolutionary transformation. Planning, either before or after the revolutionary leap, will have to transform the abstraction of knowing the tendency into the constituent potentiality [*potenza*] of future institutions that are postcapitalist and communist. It is therefore a 'planning', which – according to the Manifesto – is not vertical command exerted by the state over working-class society but has to be, today, convergence among the productive and the directing capacities in the network– this is the line of thinking that should be taken and the task to achieve: planning of the struggles before the planning of production. I shall say more about this shortly.

Let us return to us. The first thing, then, is to unleash the power of cognitive labour, plucking it out of its latency. Surely we still don't know what a modern techno-social body is capable of! Two elements need to be stressed here. One is what some call 'appropriation of fixed capital' and the consequent anthropological transformation of the labouring subject; the other element is the sociopolitical one, in other words the consideration that this new potentiality of bodies is essentially collective, political. To put it another way, one could say that the surplus, the value added in production and in the tendential development of the potentialities created by the appropriation of fixed capital, derives essentially from *social productive cooperation*. Probably this is the most important contribution of the Manifesto. With an attitude that attenuates and sometimes renders inessential the humanistic determinations of philosophical critique, the Manifesto stresses the material qualities and techniques of the *bodily* reappropriation of fixed capital. The productive quantification, the economic modelling, the 'big data' analyses, the more abstract cognitive models . . . well, all this is appropriated through education and through the scientific re-elaboration that the worker subjects give it. The fact that the mathematical models and algorithms are at the service of capital is not a quality of their own, is not a problem of mathematics – it's just a problem of power.

That there is a certain optimism here is beyond doubt: this perception cannot be very useful, for example, for the critique of the human–machine relationship (which is sometimes far more complex); and yet, even having taken on board this critique, the optimistic and slightly auroral Machiavelli helps us to dive straight into the discussion about organisation – which is very urgent today. So, given that the discourse addresses the balance of power, it leads straight into one of organisation.

In the Manifesto's view, the left has to develop a sociotechnological hegemony – 'the material platforms of production, finance, logistics and consumption can and will be reprogrammed and reformatted towards post-capitalist ends'. There is here undoubtedly a strong trust in the objectivity, materiality, one could say *Dasein* of development – and consequently a certain underestimation of social, political and cooperative elements, of the convention assumed when one adheres to the basic protocol of the 'one has split up into two' – but this underestimation should not prevent us from understanding the importance of the acquisition of the highest techniques of capitalist command, of the abstraction of labour, for bringing them back to that communist administration that sees itself as conducted 'by the things themselves'.

I understand this passage in the following way: in order to propose a new hegemony, the whole complex of the productive possibilities of cognitive labour needs to mature. And here recurs the theme of proper organisation. Against extremist horizontalism – as I have already said – it proposes a new reconfiguration of the relationship between network and planning; against any pacifist understanding of democracy as a process, an attention shifted from means (voting, representation, state of law, etc.) to ends (collective emancipation and self-government). That this should not see the rise of new centralist illusions and empty reinterpretations of the 'dictatorship of the proletariat' is self-evident. But the Manifesto appreciates the need to push the clarification forward and proposes a kind of 'ecology of organisations': that is, it insists on a pluralistic framework of forces that come into resonance with each other and in this way succeed, beyond any sectarianism, in producing motors of collective decision. One could have doubts about this proposal and recognise in it difficulties in excess of the happy options it presumes; and yet this is a path to follow, all the more clearly today, at the end of that cycle of struggles that began in 2011 and that, despite a substantial power and a proposal of new contents that are genuinely revolutionary, have nevertheless come up against insuperable limits in the clash with power – with the maintenance of that form of organisation.

The Manifesto proposes three urgent objectives, which are decidedly appropriate and realistic. First, to construct a kind of intellectual infrastructure that could build a new project of ideas and could study new economic models. Second, a strong initiative in the field of the mainstream communication media: the Internet and the social networks have undoubtedly democratised communication and can be very useful in the struggle, but this communication still remains entirely subordinate to the stronger traditional forms of communication. The idea here is to concentrate large resources and to devote all possible energies to the objective of getting people's hands on adequate means of communication. Third, the capacities to build all possible institutional forms (transient or permanent, political and trade union, global and local) of power and class must be reactivated: a unitary constitution of class power will be possible only through the assemblage and hybridisation of all the experiences thus far developed and of others yet to be had.

The future needs to be built: this Enlightenment-style request runs throughout the whole of the Manifesto. It also fully embodies a Promethean and humanist politics – but a humanism that, seeking to go beyond the limits imposed by capitalist society, opens itself to the posthuman, to scientific utopianism, by taking up (among other things) the space-exploration dreams of the twentieth century or, to give more examples, the building of ever more insurmountable bulwarks against death and against all the accidents of life. Rational imagination has to be accompanied by the collective imagination of new worlds, organising a powerful 'self-valorisation' of labour and of the social. The more modern epoch we have lived has shown us that there is only an inside of globalisation, there is no longer an outside. Today, however, by raising afresh the theme of building the future, we have the necessity, and undoubtedly also the possibility, of bringing the outside inside too, of giving the inside a mighty breathing space.

What can one say about this document? Some of us see it as a postworkerist 'complement', born in the Anglo-Saxon world, less available for repackagings of socialist humanism, more capable of developing a positive humanism. The name 'accelerationist' is somewhat unfortunate, because it gives a 'futurist' tinge to something that is not futuristic. The document undoubtedly has a feel of topicality, not only in its critique of socialism and of 'real' social democracy, but also in its analysis and critique of the movements of 2011 and of subsequent years. It raises very powerfully the question of the tendency of capitalist development, of the necessity of its reappropriation and of its rupture: in short, on this basis, it proposes the construction of a communist programme. All this gives a strong basis for going further.

A few points of criticism could be useful for reopening the discussion and for pushing the argument and the agreement forward. The first is that there is a little too much determinism, not only technological but also political, in this project. The relation to historicity (or, if you prefer, to history, to present realities, to praxis) risks being distorted by something that one would not wish to call teleology but that looks like it. The relation to singularity – and therefore to the ability to view the tendency as a virtuality (which involves singularities) and the material determination (which pushes forward the tendency) as a potentiality [*potenza*] of subjectivity – seems to me to have been undervalued. The tendency cannot be defined except as an open relationship, as a constitutive relationship, animated by class subjects. It could be objected that this insistence on openness can produce perverse effects, for example a picture so heterogeneous as to allow itself to be defined as chaotic and therefore non-resolvable; a multiplicity magnified to the point of constituting a bad infinity. This is undoubtedly what postworkerism, or even *Mille plateaux*, can sometimes suggest. This is a difficult point to deal with, but is crucial. Let's dig into it a little deeper.

It is true that the Manifesto is armed with a good solution for this purpose when, right at the centre of the relationship between subject and object (we, accustomed to other terminologies, would call it a relationship between the technical and the political composition of the proletariat), it makes a transformative anthropology of the bodies of the workers decide on this intersection. That is how the hazards of pluralism could be avoided. But it is also true that, if we want to proceed in this area – which I believe is useful, in fact decisive – we also have to break at some point that relentless progression of the productive tension that the Manifesto indicates: we have to determine a number of 'thresholds' in development – thresholds that consist of the consolidation – as Deleuze and Guattari would say – of *agencements collectifs* in the reappropriation of fixed capital and in the transformation of labour power, of anthropology and languages and activities. These thresholds are those that arise in the relationship between the technical composition and political composition of the proletariat and they are fixed historically. Without these consolidations, a programme, however transitory, is impossible. And it is precisely because we are unable today to define such a relationship with precision that we find ourselves sometimes methodologically helpless and politically powerless. In contrast, it is the determination of a historical threshold and the awareness of a specific modality of the technical–political relationship that permits the formulation of an organisational process and the definition of an appropriate programme.

Mind you, when this problem is formulated, there arises, implicitly (if one accepts the progressive nature of the tendency in production), the problem of better defining the process in which the relationship between singularities and the common grows and consolidates. We need to specify *how much of the common* there is in every technological connection by developing a deeper approach, specifically in the anthropology of production.

Again we are back to this matter of the reappropriation of fixed capital. I have already remarked that in the Manifesto the cooperative dimension of production (and especially the production of subjectivity) is undervalued in relation to the criteria of technology, to the importance of the material aspects that, apart from being parameters of productivity, also constitute the anthropological transformations of labour power. I stress this point. It is in relation to the ensemble of languages and algorithms, of technological functions and know-how within which today's proletariat is actually formed that the element of cooperation becomes central and an indicator of possible hegemony. This statement derives from the observation that the very structure of capitalist exploitation has now been modified. Capital continues to exploit, but does so in forms that are paradoxically limited by comparison to its potential [*potenza*] for extracting surplus labour from the whole of society. When we understand this new determination, we realise that fixed capital, in other words that part of capital that is directly involved in the production of surplus value, refers to, or rather is established primarily in, *the surplus created out of cooperation*. And this surplus is the non-measurable something that, as Marx said, does not consist of the sum of two or more workers' surplus labour but of the 'plus' that derives from the fact that they work together (in short, the 'plus' that goes beyond the sum). If one assumes the pre-eminence of extractive capital over the capital that exploits (naturally including the latter in the former), one arrives at some very interesting conclusions. Here is one. Once upon a time people described the transition from Fordism to post-Fordism by characterising it as the application of 'automation' in the factory and the management of 'computerisation' in the social domain. The latter is of great importance in the process that leads to the complete (real) subsumption of society to capital – informatics interprets and conducts the tendency. And it is, one might say, more important than automation, which, in that transition, succeeds in characterising the new form of society only with difficulty, by investing partially and precariously in the mode of production. Today, as the Manifesto spells out well and as experience teaches us, we are well beyond that transition. It is not just that productive society appears to be globally computerised, but this social world of informatics is itself reorganised in automatic terms, according to new criteria in the division of labour (in the management of the labour market), and by new hierarchical parameters in the management of society. In short, when production becomes generalised throughout society – through cognitive labour, through social knowledge – computerisation undoubtedly remains the fixed capital most prized by capitalism; but automation – and I give this name to the technological structuring of direct productive command, which intervenes not simply inside the factory any more but also in the social activity of the producers – becomes the cement of capitalist organisation, which bends in its favour both informatics, by making it

a tool, and digital society, which it seeks to turn into a machinic pros-
thesis of command over production. Information technologies thus
come to be subordinated to automation. The command of capitalist
algorithms marks this transformation of command over production.
We are at a higher level of real subsumption. From this derives the
enormous importance of logistics, which – when it is automated –
begins to configure every territorial dimension of capitalist command
and to establish internal boundaries and hierarchies of global space;
and also the importance of all the algorithmic mechanisms that
concentrate and command, by degrees of abstraction and branches
of expertise, with frequent and functional variants, that complex
of forms of knowledge otherwise called 'general intellect'. Now, if
extractive capitalism widens 'extensively' its ability to take advantage
of all social infrastructure and applies itself 'intensively' to every
degree of abstraction in the production machine, that is, to each level
in the organisation of the global financial mode of production, at this
point one has to reopen debate on the appropriation of fixed capital
over this entire space, theoretical and practical. The construction of
struggles has to be on the scale of this space. Fixed capital can in fact
be potentially appropriated by the proletarians. It is this potentiality
that has to be liberated.

One last point, which is underplayed in the Manifesto but is entirely
consistent with the theory developed therein – the money of the
common. It certainly does not escape the authors of the Manifesto
that, as an abstract machine, money has assumed today the unique
function of supreme measuring device of the values extracted from
society in the real subsumption of society to capital. Now, the same
schema that leads to the extraction or exploitation of social labour in
its highest expression makes us recognise that money is there – money
as measure, money as hierarchy, money as plan. But, insofar as this
monetary abstraction is the tendential result of financial capital's
becoming hegemonic, it points to the potentiality of forms of resistance and subversion at the same very high level. It is on this terrain
that the communist programme for a postcapitalist future needs to
be elaborated, not only by proposing the proletarian reappropriation
of wealth but also by constructing its hegemonic capacity – that is, by
working on that common that is the basis of the highest extraction–
abstraction of the value of labour and also of its universal translation
into money. Today this means 'the money of the common' – nothing
utopian but rather a paradigmatic and programmatic indication of
how to prefigure, in the struggle, the attack against the measure
of labour imposed by capital, against the hierarchies of articulation

between necessary labour and surplus labour (imposed by the direct boss), and against the general distribution of social income commanded by the capitalist state. On this perspective we still have a lot of work to do.

And, to conclude (there are still so many things worth exploring!): What does it mean to follow through the tendency right to the end and to beat capital in this process? To take just one example: today it means renewing the slogan of 'refusal of work'. The struggle against the algorithmic automaton must grasp positively the increase in productivity that this automaton brings about; it must therefore impose drastic reductions in the time of employment, which is disciplined and controlled by or within the machines for each worker – and there must be substantial wage increases, always more substantial. On the one hand, the time of service at the automaton will have to be regulated in a manner that is equal for all (in the postcapitalist era – but this means immediately formulating in this direction the objectives of struggle). On the other hand, a substantial citizen income will have to translate every figure of service work into the recognition that all participate equally in the building of collective wealth. In this way all persons will be able to develop freely and to the full their *joie de vivre* (to rehearse here Marx's appreciation for Fourier). This, too, has to be fought for immediately, through struggle. But here one would have to open another subject: that of the production of subjectivity, that of the agonist usage of the passions and of historical dialectics, which this usage opens against capitalist and sovereign command.

Toni Negri
7 February 2014

16

Notes on the Abstract Strike

What was the strike? It was a withdrawal from work by workers, an unruly and partisan (working class) breakpoint in the relationship of exploitation, and it was seen as a direct attack on capitalist exploitation. But from the working-class point of view the strike was not only this; it was also something very material, an action that had to 'hurt the bosses' and that at the same time put the workers' lives on the line. There was something carnal, something immediately biopolitical in the strike, a violence that transformed economic action into political representation and the act of withdrawal into a practice of desertion from capital. Now we know that the nature of the capital relation changes over time, both because the worker-subject at each stage of capitalist development has different characteristics and because the command over labour differs according to context. Hence the strike also changes: the strikes of industrial workers and those of agricultural workers were very different experiences, very different adventures, even though each brought into play the same materiality – the continuity of sabotage and of prolonged withdrawal from work in the case of the industrial workers; the carnal, focused, and very harsh violence of peasant struggles. For agricultural workers, the struggle could continue only for so long: they tell of desperate cattle mooing when nobody was around to milk them, of harvests that were left uncollected and went to rot – so they had to intensify the struggle over a short time span. For industrial workers, the timings and styles of the struggle were very different and did not need to be shortened, except in the final instance, by the limit that the measure of the necessary wage – the survival wage – imposed on withdrawal from work. But, in the bosses' view of things, the strike is one single reality (an economic breach of the relationship of valorisation and a political breach of subordination) and its variety is cancelled out in an act of repression that always has political and highly symbolic motivations: order has to be reimposed. When neoliberalism was inaugurated in the 1980s as a general plan for transformations in labour, in the form of production, and in the political control of the working class, we know that the answer to the struggles of the mass-worker had already been given through the automation of the factory and through the computerisation of society: indeed the basis for the success of neoliberalism was precisely cybernetic entrepreneurship. But this transformation of control was introduced by a symbolic act, a political act that says that the bosses now know – wherever, whenever, and unrelentingly – how to resist the working-class attack. The repression of the miners' strike by Margaret Thatcher and Ronald Reagan's attack on the air traffic controllers – these manifest themselves as a necessary precondition for the transformation of the mode of production. Here the symbolic character – later to be called 'biopolitical' – of the repression of struggles appears in its extreme violence, pushing out of the picture all possible notions of negotiation. The working-class strike is now confronted by 'biopower'.

To move the analysis forward and deal with the question of the 'abstract strike' we need to ask the question: Who is now the worker and who is now the boss? First, who is the worker? The worker is someone who operates in an immaterial network – made up of the workers themselves but controlled by a boss – which at the same time enhances the workers' productivity and extracts value from them. These are workers who, growing within a more and more intense cooperation, manifest an increasing productive capacity and understand their labour power as a motive power [*potenza*] of the production system. Let me explain: within cooperation, labour becomes increasingly 'abstract' and hence increasingly capable of organising production, but at the same time increasingly subjected to mechanisms of extraction of value: able to create cooperation in production and obliged to see it extracted (by capital) to an increasingly high degree. To get to understand this process, one should stress above all that, in relation to machinery, the worker develops more and more autonomously the aspect of cooperation and in this way organises the productive energy that has been expressed. Can we speak of autonomy here in the same sense as we did at other stages of the formal or real subsumption of labour under capital? Certainly not. Because here there is a degree of autonomy that is not simply one of position but is ontological – an autonomous consistency, even if completely subjected to capitalist command. What does it mean to be in a situation where a continuous (over time) and extended (in space) productive initiative, and a collective and cooperating power of invention, are extracted by capital? When the relation between the labour process (in the hands of the workers) and the capitalist process of value creation changes and they become separated, the former being entrusted to the autonomy of living labour and the latter to pure command – what does this change mean? It means that labour has reached a level of dignity and strength that refuses to accept the form of exploitation imposed on it – and therefore, albeit still within the imposition of command, is capable of developing its own autonomy.

In the unbridled propaganda of capitalist command and of its inevitability, in the latest sermons on the efficacy without alternatives of the power of capital that the 'one-track thinking' ['*pensiero unico*'] of the bosses and of the social democrats like to flaunt – we hear them more and more singing praises to the domination of the 'algorithm'. But what is this algorithm, to which is attributed today control over the processes of IT valorisation [*valorizzazione informatica*]? It is nothing but a machine, a machine that is born from the cooperation of the workers and that the bosses then impose over this cooperation. The algorithm is, in the words of our old friend Marx, a machine that runs to the place where there is strike action, wherever there is resistance or a breach of the valorisation process – a machine produced today by that same power and autonomy that is expressed by living labour. The big difference between the labour processes studied by Marx and the current ones is that cooperation today is no longer imposed by the boss but produced 'from within' the workforce; that the production process and the machines are not brought 'from the outside' by the boss, nor are the workers forcibly obliged. Today we can properly speak of an appropriation of fixed capital by the workers and refer by this to a process – for example, of construction of the cognitive algorithm – that is disposed to the valorisation of labour in all of its articulations and capable of producing languages of which it will become the master [*dominus*]. Those languages are thus created by the workers who hold their key and their engine of cooperation.

If this is how things are, it is only by increasingly abstracting itself from the labour processes that capitalist command is able to function. It is not by chance that we speak of an 'extractive exploitation' of social cooperation, and no longer of an exploitation tied to the industrial and temporal dimensions of the organisation of labour. In this type of organisation of labour and of valorisation, a complex but basically linear role is therefore being played out: one of the 'production of subjectivity', where by 'production of subjectivity' I mean on the one hand a production through 'subjectivation' and, on the other, a continuous effort to reduce the latter to a commanded 'subject'. The ambiguity that this game presents is the same as that of all the different figures of living labour in its postindustrial structuration.

Second, what is the boss today? In relation to cognitive labour, bosses present themselves in the form of finance capital that *extracts* social value. Within this 'extraction' a process is now under way, namely a progressive reduction of the boss function from an entrepreneurial category to a purely political category. The verticalisation of capitalist command must cross, in an increasingly abstract manner, the relationship with cooperation and the processes of productive subjectivation – consequently, within this verticalisation, a kind of 'governmentalisation' of command will be expressed: the increasingly complex attempt to control the machinic–algorithmic mechanisms through which living labour has proposed cooperation and constructed it. From this perspective, finance capital presents itself as 'dictatorship' – not a fascist dictatorship, of course, but an abstraction of command and its governmental uniformisation, in the attempt to establish its authority over the process of abstraction – in short, to match *extraction* with *abstraction*.

In studying the new type of capitalist command, one should distinguish two aspects. I have already stated the first: abstract–extractive command and its claim to recuperate the entire process of value creation. This is where political command organises itself. But alongside this there is the other aspect: neoliberalism is, in its own way, constituent. In addition to developing a governing activity that is only command – basically financial, but backed by the highest state force – it develops through networks (with multiple forms of governmentality) and acts as participatory command over an extensive micropolitical network inclined to encompass needs and desires. The neoliberal constitution does not simply gather (and extract value from) living labour in its valorising expression; it also tends to organise consumption and desires in order to make them, in their material expression, reproductive, cooperative, and functional for the reproduction of capital. It is *money* that, in the age of finance capital, mediates between production and consumption, between needs and capitalist reproduction, and therefore equalises and collects into one single abstraction the labour that produces it and the labour that consumes it. Will it be possible to traverse this complex, reappropriating to ourselves the labour that produces and liberating consumption from its capitalist management?

When, twenty years ago, we began talking in terms of 'immaterial labour', we were derided not only because we were saying (incorrectly) 'immaterial', when of course all labour is material, but especially because through that immateriality we meant acts that were constitutive of value, of knowledge, of languages, of desires – and not simply manual labour. Today, of course, they can no longer mock – it is obvious to all that we are in a situation where capital has fully identified that new and very rich context in which living labour expresses itself and has placed it entirely under its command. Capital has acted in two directions. On the one hand, it has articulated its command to the living production of languages; on the other hand, it operates by making needs and desires functional to capitalist command. Capital (in neoliberalism) wants the power of productive *subjectivation* to be recognised as a *subject* of the capital relationship. It wants voluntary servitude. This ambiguity is pushed to the limit: just as there is no production without living labour, likewise, there is no value creation (or reproduction) without consumption. Keynesianism, albeit unrecognisable, is explicitly internalised and renewed in the neoliberal constitution – hence the impotent mystifications often produced or suffered by too many people who are honest but incapable of critical judgement: it is argued that capital is now able to make happy those who are dominated. What we have here is a recantation of servitude that masquerades as truth. I, however, prefer to think that to live in capital is necessarily to resist it.

What is an abstract strike today? Put another way: What kind of strike can measure itself both in relation to the new nature of living labour and in relation to the neoliberal constitution of production and reproduction? What kind of social struggle has the ability to 'hurt' the system, to manifest itself once again with a material, biopolitical and efficacious power [*potenza*]? To answer these questions, I should stress two points that cannot be separated but are useful to distinguish. First, we have to ask ourselves whether and how living labour today can rebel and interrupt the flow of valorisation. The answer to this question has to take on board the entire tradition of working-class struggle: the breakdown of the relationship of production, withdrawal, sabotage, exodus, and so on. But – you may say – when work has invested the whole of life, when you work all day outside of any timetable, when the productive capacities of each worker are caught in networks of command – how is it possible to regain that independence of action (which is required by the act of 'going on strike') both on the terrain of spatial links of cooperation and on that of temporal links, which are now reduced to a continuous flow? How is it possible, for example, to occupy and block the metropolis (which has become productive) or to interrupt that flow of social network productivity that can never stop? Here the answer cannot but bring us back to that singular composition that is represented today by the intimate algorithmic connection between production and command: to the place where workers build meaningful and productive relationships whose value is then extracted by capital. In this case the strike can succeed not just when it breaks the process of valorisation but when it recovers the independence, the consistency of living labour, when it becomes a productive act. In the strike, machinic living labour breaks the algorithm in order to build new networks of signification. Not only can it do that – because, without production by living labour, without subjectivation, there is no algorithm; it has to do it – because in capitalism without resistance there is no wage, no social promotion, no welfare, no possible enjoyment of life. The strike reveals the future, breaking with the misery and the subjection to command – hence the strike as recovery of a working-class tradition extended over the whole terrain of life – the *social strike*. This is the symbol of the strike against capitalist techniques that extract the value of society as a whole.

But there is a second point of attack, which is just as important, or perhaps even more: it is where the processes of reproduction of society intersect with finance capital, with the monetisation of the process. Here it is clear that we need to break and reconstruct the mechanism that links consumption to the monetary dimension. Consumption is always a good thing when one is able to consume in relation to the needs of reproduction of the species – not so much the needs of the natural, generic human species as those of the working-class species, the productive species, the 'posthuman' species. And it is this kind of consumption that should be taken as a moment of rupture. Now this is the terrain of welfare (the locus of the organisation of domination over services and consumption), which should be traversed as a terrain of struggle – of exercising resistance and of developing alternative prospects. The abstract strike becomes here a materialist strike. The issue is to retrieve, for living labour, command over consumption and to build or impose a 'production of humans for humans' and not for profit.

At the level of production, then, the abstract strike involves regaining the independence of living labour in order to break the process of valorisation; at the level of reproduction, it requires the construction and imposition of a new sequence of needs–desires–consumptions. Characteristic to our present times is the abundance of research committed to the attempt (and sometimes increasing the tension around it) to build spaces of independence at work within production networks that are the ones most invested by the capitalist capacity to extract value. The revival of mutualism and the growth of cooperation across digital networks are just the first steps of struggle that need to be deepened. As regards the breaking of the desires–consumptions sequence (and their enforced monetisation), interesting attempts are being made to create bit money and to build autonomous networks of communication and independent networks of consumption – attempts that are partial but significant. However, their effectiveness will not become decisive unless these initiatives connect with one another and offensively grasp that crucial point at which capitalist production transforms productive subjectivation into an autocratic production of subjects. It is obvious that political democracy is incompatible with the dictatorship of finance capital. The *abstract strike* makes this assumption in order to indicate a number of terrains on which it is necessary to intervene in order to build an independent power [*potenza*] capable of proposing and making possible another, democratic world.

To conclude: it is clear that the strike against the extraction of value and the strike that moves at the level of capitalist abstraction of social exploitation are not the same thing. In the first case the struggle is aimed at the appropriation of profit (or at a distribution of profit that is more favourable to the workers); in the second case it aims at overturning (1) the models of reproduction of society and of its capitalist rule and (2) the contextual functional minting of money. So it is clear that today, while these two levels of struggle are not identical, they are very much related to each other. One is *horizontal*, the other is *vertical*. One is the struggle for the emancipation *of* labour, the other is the struggle for liberation *from* labour. But, from the point of view of the struggles, it is hard to tell them apart. Yet they cannot be confused either – and the reason is to be found in everything that has been said thus far, because one struggles and the other *constructs*. They have to do this separately, but they have to do it together. This is the task at hand. So much for the analysis; next comes the praxis. So it is clear that, while neoliberalism imposes the dictatorship of finance capital, the struggle for the liberation of and from work – the communist struggle – requires the existence of coalitions of workers who carry out the struggle on the horizontal terrain, against extractive exploitation, and are able to rise to the [task of] producing a project alternative to capital's management – [a project] of extracting value, but above all of [imposing] measure: of money. Here we come up against dictatorship. The comrades of Syriza today, those of Podemos tomorrow: this is where they have brought the struggle – to the crossroads between the emancipation *of* labour and liberation *from* labour. Will Italy succeed in building a coalition of workers that is similarly powerful?

Toni Negri
Venice, 8 May 2015

17

From the Factory to the Metropolis . . . and Back Again

The transition from extraction of surplus value in the factory to extraction of surplus value that operates in the metropolis is a subject that I have already covered in this book. But what about the return journey? From the metropolis to the factory? Where, how, what does this mean? And what has happened to the subject, the person who produces, the bearer of living labour? What has that person become in this transition? What are the characteristics of the exploited metropolitan worker, and in what respect is this person differentiated (or not) from the factory worker? Does the metropolitan common permit the insertion, in its own movement, of a new form of exploitation and of a new type of the proletariat (cognitive, in this instance)? Let's start with this last question, by underlining the most obvious differences between the current and the preceding situation.

That the common was always present in the construction and in the definition of the city is obvious. When Max Weber defines the city as the birthplace of the bourgeoisie and as the centre of the conceptualisation of the modern, this foundational concept is by itself open to the cooperation of singularities, to the common. From its very birth, the city is an expression of the multitude: of an *associated multitude that produces* – not only in the spaces left free by private or public ownership but by traversing the places of coexistence, by filling or emptying them, depending on the political circumstances of the city. It is clear, then, that the common presents itself as the other face of the political in the institutional system of the city; where the political shifts between the private and the public, the common is the basis of this shifting and constitutes its ontological foundation. (Here as throughout this book, may I take the drama out of the term 'ontological', please: to me it means simply the context, the historical accumulation, that mobile reality on which we can firmly place our feet.) An archaeology of the common has no choice but to pass through the history of the city. And a genealogy can only be achieved in the projection – whether real or ideal – of the common of the city, or rather of the metropolis of the common.

The first thing that appears to me clearly in the great transformation that has taken place in the past fifty years is that our metropolitan lifestyles are utterly different from those of the previous generations. The life of the metropolis has changed substantially; its timings have become pluralised, and every custom and former regularity has been interrupted. Life in the city has *accelerated* through this dissolution of any rule, through this elimination of any intermediate space and of any disconnected temporality. And yet, for every moment of rupture on record, a new connection to the totality of the urban movement is now determined – through replacement, through superposition, through supplementation; a connection that is fluid and controllable, malleable and totalising. For example, the working day is no longer eight hours; it is now twenty-four, and any of the spaces that make up this duration can be increased or decreased, subtracted or incremented. This new compactness of temporality is produced over and through a desynchronisation, and it is the ability or power of intervention on this latter phenomenon that has recomposed the metropolitan cycle of production. It is not only the timetable in the factories that has changed, but also the timetable of all forms of work, with entirely new consequences. Take domestic workers (or women doing housework) or women working in supermarkets – they have completely discontinuous schedules. But this discontinuity – which is heightened by variables pertaining to everyday life and to means of transportation – is generally recomposed after it has appeared as an element of real social need, taking into account the imperative of social dialogue and the calculation of the biopolitical costs. This regulation mechanism is mystified under the categories of negotiation of the common and the institutions' maximum commitment to produce social cooperation: if only that were true!

From the moment the metropolis became a factory, it also came to be organised by a 'machinic structure'. This structure constitutes the body of the metropolis: the body of the 'urban whole'. Many fantasies have developed around the perception of this 'whole'. It has sometimes been defined as a machinic, comprehensive and concentric totality; other times as a corporeal totality, intelligent and diffuse. In fact, far from being 'scientific', these definitions are born as tools for the governance of the city: they portray the metropolis as a cybernetic city in order to permit a technocratic management of it. But this is merely sleight of hand! For good reason, authors gifted with critical qualities (Adam Greenfield in particular) have no problem in showing that this way of looking at the city is a kind of unrepentant logical positivism that supposes the urban world to be perfectly knowable, its contents measurable, and its relationships meaningful and encodable without bias. From this angle it is not surprising that a sort of algebraic (and algorithmic) analytics comes to be used as a tool for understanding complexity and superimposes itself on the plural and varied reality of the city. No, this is not an adequate tool.

And not only because, behind the compactness of capitalist command, the metropolis is a multiple and jumbled ensemble of actions and behaviours, but also because – as has already been said – in it is revealed that 'common' – hidden but powerful – that traverses both private actions and public interventions. It is not possible to break free from this force: it is a constant accompaniment of our lives. It is systematically mystified and privately appropriated, owned by the public and paraded as 'general interest' – in fact it presents itself as the collective experience of a force that, over time, may be communitarian or antagonist, destructive or constructive. Within the urban dimension the desire of the 'common' is born as a search for spaces that are available for 'use', serviceable and tailored to the 'good life'.

Some say that we should leave the city, that this complexity is stifling. No, we cannot live *outside* the city, we cannot free ourselves from common exploitation except through collective action – through the 'insurrection of the common'. We cannot liberate ourselves from complexity to seek autonomy, solitude or – worse – simply to limit consumption (what a stupid rhetoric!). We have to invest the complexity, reorganising it and bringing it back to the 'common'. The machinic system that traverses the city is not just a coercive way of fencing in – like in a science fiction film – the conducts of the singularities, but rather a space of conflict, of enjoyment in struggle, and also of suffering in being exploited, repressed and defeated; *but in there is where we are*. As it is for power, as it is for capital, the machinic system or the algorithm of the metropolis is twofold, broken in two. Yes, it is represented by the intimate algorithmic connection between production and command – that is, where workers or citizens build meaningful and productive relationships whose value is extracted by capital. But resistance happens when it breaks the process of valorisation (in the *resistance*, certainly, but often also solely by its *existence*) and thus recovers the independence and consistency of living labour.

Machinic living labour breaks the algorithm through resistance and builds new networks of meaning. It can do this because, without production by living labour, without subjectivation, there is not even the algorithm. It has to do this because, without resistance, there is neither capitalism, nor wage, nor social promotion, nor any possible enjoyment of life. In the metropolis only resistance reveals the future of our singularities, breaking with the misery of the citizens or workers and their subjection to command. We cannot free ourselves from that machinic body but we can make use of it, bringing ourselves close to enjoyment. The category of 'use' is central here.

At this point it is worth opening a long parenthesis on 'use' – on use value and exchange value. (I refer the reader to the discussion developed in my other writings: *Marx Beyond Marx: Lessons on the* Grundrisse, Bergin & Garvey Publishers, South Hadley, MA, 1984; *Time for Revolution*, Continuum, London and New York, 2005. Here I shall limit myself to a few observations.) It is evident that, in capitalist development, any 'use', any use value was reduced under the category of exchange. Recovering 'use' as a 'form of life' will therefore mean breaking the coercive link, the violence (contractual or exceptional) that clings to it. The metropolitan struggles – what we call today 'social strike' (see above, Chapter 16) – are an effective weapon on this terrain. We should not find it surprising, then, that, in the current urbanist utopia, that of the antagonistic militants in the architecture profession, people are now taking up models such as the 'closed fortress', which workers sought to create for their own neighbourhoods in Vienna in the early twentieth century. They are also picking up on the idea of 'Bigness' that Rem Koolhaas had developed, as a model for a place where the multitude can live and autonomously recompose itself. It is no accident that the Florentine workerists [*operaisti*] of Archizoom have been working on this imaginary and have been at the centre of the ensuing debate.

All this has a subjective correlate. We have to 'urbanise technologies', says Saskia Sassen. What does this mean, if not that we have to democratise intelligence? And that we have to find operationally, in the metropolis, the dimension of the common? But what is this dimension, if not a production of subjectivity? Already the recompositional dynamic that brings the various figures of labour together under the sign of general intellect, of cognitive labour power, of cooperative interrelation requires at the same time that the traditional sectors of administration of the city (transport, construction, green spaces, roads, energy and leisure) be reunited – or rather transformed into new, complex types of service, or (better) into productions of the metropolitan cooperation of citizens. In fact the city is permanently traversed – especially since it became productive and an indisputable high point in the production of value – by trajectories of innovation. The problem will no longer be how to describe them, but how to entrust the citizens or workers, from below, with the function of becoming conscious of them and of governing the system.

Taking up the insights of Henri Lefebvre, David Harvey has understood, right from the start of his work on building the concept of 'extractive exploitation', that the city was the product of a living labour power – and that it was this overall product that was expropriated by capital. But today is the time to return anew to the city, to reconsider it through the activities of the people who inhabit it, through the common that is interpreted in this way – in short, by filtering knowledge through the entire projection of (the operation on) social relations. Henri Lefebvre lived the last phase of Fordism – when the city seemed on the verge of its definitive subordination to the rules of that external power that was industry, with its relentlessly rigid serial organisation of the 'working day'. The 'working day' that Marx had studied and that all the great novelists of the late nineteenth century had told us about, after having imposed a machinic command on the metropolis, was now in crisis – when it was not actually on the point of being destroyed. The working-class *cités* that surrounded the metropolis and constituted its adjoining productive machine were experiencing an initial degradation and began to be reduced to dustbins [*poubelles*]. The 'fiscal crisis of the city' pushed away from its centres the 'creative classes' of the time, actually the well-to-do bourgeoisie. The Lefebvrian utopia consisted in subjecting this crisis to the test of proletarian resistances, and thus not only in rediscovering the centrality of the metropolis but also in foreseeing the recovery of its productive potential [*potenza*] in the near future. And this is what happened. As it recovered a productive function – not simply an administrative function of impoverished peripheries condemned to factory work – and as it became rather the central point of the production of subjectivity, the city was considered by Lefebvre a new moment of creative effervescence and a political space that could represent a radical democratic value. The class struggle reinserted itself into the city and gave it a new, decisive importance for the fate of our free and civil living. It was no longer the city of the bourgeoisie but the metropolis of the cognitive worker, of the young and precarious proletariat that was invading it: a new potential [*potenziale*] of the 'common' that was entering into the metropolis.

Are we witnessing the fulfilment of Lefebvre's prediction, the enactment of his dystopia? There is no doubt that living in, occupying – from squats to the street demonstrations of 2011, from Occupy to the experiences of self-administration, cooperation and construction of 'liberated zones' – is rediscovering itself as a communard practice, antiliberalist and ecological. Mutual aid and cooperation now always arise when transformation imposes itself and when crisis is just around the corner. The struggle against real estate rent becomes central in the political self-realisation of the citizens or workers. Extractive entrepreneurship is countered by a resistance that assumes as its base the common: *the right of use of the common*. Income, welfare and citizenship become the battlefields on which housing and habitation serve as a trench, as a place of resistance (often as a place in which debt and poverty are found coexisting, but also from where they will be expelled). The initiatives of mutualisation and the calls for a citizen's income are the new fronts of anticapitalism, demands matched to the needs of 'being a citizen'. Not 'having' but 'being', not an ownership but a work, an activity, not a private appropriation or a public use but the construction of the common.

Let me summarise here and lay down a few basic points. Today, when we address the question of the metropolis in crisis, on the one hand we discover its productive centrality, now renewed (after a long period of transition); on the other hand we rediscover the new role of the citizen or worker. Often this person is *the poor*. But any analysis of poverty today has to develop on a terrain that concedes nothing to the past: in the transition to postmodernity – from the slavery of Fordism to finance capitalism, from the Taylorised slave to the knowledge worker – we are moving on a completely new terrain. In the metropolis, the multitude is fighting against poverty even as it creates the common wealth directly – since it has reappropriated for itself the tools of production, which have become intellectual. The city is the fundamental place of this battle. Marx deepened the first trajectory of this critique, but most of all he revealed its logic. The capitalist form of poverty is given, as I have said, in the long and complex process of 'primitive accumulation' of capital – which is being renewed today, in other forms, in the metropolis. After having been separated from the land and from all independent means of production, the workers are 'free' in a double sense: free because they are no longer subordinated to relations of feudal serfdom, and free in the sense that they no longer have any property or any legal right to own land. The proletariat is being created as multitude of the poor. *De te fabula narratur* ['You are the subject of the story']: the same process repeats itself in the metropolis today in the transition from industrial labour to cognitive labour. The multitude of the poor is the multitude of cognitive workers. But Marx counters that the capacity for labour, stripped of the means of labour and means of subsistence, is thus absolute poverty; and the worker, as a simple personification of it, according to Marx's concept, is *the poor*. The poor of whom he is speaking is not simply the person who lives in poverty at the limits of survival, but all workers whose living labour is separated from the objectified labour destined for capital accumulation – and today this is fundamentally the case in the metropolis. Here Marx obviously correlates the poverty of the proletariat to its potentiality [*potenza*], in the sense that living labour is the general possibility of material wealth in capitalist society. There is here an explosive mixture of power [*potenza*] and poverty that represents a mortal threat at the heart of private property. In the postindustrial phase of capitalist development, the separation of labour from command has increased massively, and the alienation of productive labour (intellectual, cognitive) has reached extreme heights, being embodied in the workers' proletarianisation and in the insecurity of their life. The mixture of poverty and potentiality [*potenza*] is increasingly explosive. In the metropolis, all of this is hugely magnified.

There is no longer poverty *outside* the common production of this society, outside the extraction of value accumulated in the metropolis. For example, there is no qualitative difference between the poor and the employed workers. There is instead a condition that is increasingly common to all the multitude and pertains to existence and to creative activities. The creativity and the inventiveness of the poor, of the unemployed, of the semi-employed and of the migrants are absolutely essential for social production. To the extent that production takes place today within as much as outside the factory walls, in the metropolis, it also takes place both inside and outside the wage relations. There is no social barrier between productive workers and so-called unproductive workers: both kinds participate in the metropolitan process of production. For this reason, those old, ambiguous Marxist distinctions should be definitively rejected – for instance the notion of the 'industrial reserve army'. Those hierarchies have generally been used to exclude women, the unemployed and the poor from the significant political roles that, along with revolutionary projects, were entrusted to the 'horny-handed labourers' of the big factories, in other words to those who were considered to be the producers par excellence. But how could you exclude women, the unemployed and the poor from metropolitan production today?

The struggles of the poor against the conditions of their poverty are not only forms of contestation; they are above all affirmative modalities of a biopolitical power that reveals itself as a common 'being' much more powerful than their pitiful 'having'. In the course of the twentieth century, in the dominant parts of the world, the movements of the poor populations have demonstrated the strength to overcome the fragmentation, the discouragement, the resignation and the panic that accompany poverty and have challenged national governments with their demands for wealth redistribution and with their migrations to the big metropolises. The metropolises have supplied a territory for these struggles at the global level. The metropolis is the weaving together of a common production and at the same time its product.

So, in conclusion: the class struggle has returned to the stage. It is a fight against poverty and for the construction of the common, and it unfolds in the metropolis. *The worker returns to the metropolis and opposes the common to command.*

Origin of the Texts

1. The Reappropriation of Public Space

   First published as 'Réappropriations de l'espace public', in *Futur antérieur*, 33/34, 1 (1996), at http://www.multitudes.net/ Reappropriations-de-l-espace. This is a translation from an unpublished Italian version.

2. Midway Terrains

   Translation of 'Terreni di mezzo', in *Posse: Politica filosofia moltitudini: Il lavoro di Genova, L'universo della formazione*, October 2001, pp. 197–207.

3. The Multitude and the Metropolis: A Few Notes in the Form of Hypotheses for an Inquiry into the Precariat of Global Cities

   Translation of 'Mappe politiche della multitudine', in *Posse: Politica filosofia moltitudini: Dispositivo metropoli*, October 2002, pp. 309–17. The article is archived online at https://www.mail-archive.com/rekombinant@autistici.org/msg00105.html

4. Exiting from Industrial Capitalism

   Translation of a review of Carlo Vercellone, ed., *Reditto di cittadinanza come dispositivo costituente 'intermezzo'* [*Citizen Income as an 'Intermediary' Constituent Mechanism*], in *Posse: Politica filosofia moltitudini: Movimenti costituenti*, November 2003, pp. 75–83.

5. From the Factory to the Metropolis

Translation of 'La rappresentazione impossibile', in *Posse: Politica filosofia moltitudini: Movimenti, metropoli, e autogoverno,* April 2006, pp. 96–111.

6. Metropolis and Multitude: Inquiry Notes on Precarity in Global Cities

Originally published as 'Mappe politiche della moltitudine'. The final part of this article has been rewritten for the present book.

7. Banlieue and City: A Philosophical Overview (co-authored with Jean-Marie Vincent)

Translation of 'Banlieue et ville: Un regard philosophique'. In *Futur antérieur,* 30/31/32, 4 (1995), at http://www.multitudes. net/Banlieue-et-ville-un-regard

8. Democracy versus Rent

Translation of 'La democrazia contro la rendita', in *Nota per Multitudes,* 32 2007 (27 November)

9. Presentation of Rem Koolhaas' 'Junkspace'

Translation of 'Presentazione di Junkspace di Rem Koolhaas', in Antonio Negri, *Dalla fabbrica alla metropli: saggi politici* (Rome: Datanews, 2008), pp. 213–20.

10. The Capital–Labour Relation in Cognitive Capitalism (co-authored with Carlo Vercellone)

Translation of Antonio Negri and Carlo Vercellone, 'Il rapporto capitale/lavoro nel capitalismo cognitivo' in *Posse: Politica filosofia moltitudini,* October 2007, pp. 46–56.

11. Inventing the Common of Humanity (co-authored with Judith Revel)

Translation of Judith Revel and Toni Negri, 'Inventer le common des hommes', in *Multitudes,* 31 (2007), pp. 5–10.

12. The Commune of Social Cooperation: Interview with Federico Tomasello on Questions Regarding the Metropolis

Translation of 'La Comune della cooperazione sociale: Intervista ad Antonio Negri sulla metropoli'. Posted on 25 April 2014 on EuroNomade at http://www.euronomade.info/?p=2185

13. The Common Lung of the Metropolis: Interview with Federico Tomasello

Translation of 'Il polmone comune della metropolis: Intervista ad Antonio Negri in guisa di appendice a la Comune della cooperazione sociale'. Posted on 21 July 2014 on EuroNomade at http://www.euronomade.info/?p=2675

14. The Habitat of General Intellect: A Dialogue between Antonio Negri and Federico Tomasello on Living in the Contemporary Metropolis

Translation of 'L'abitazione del general intellect: Dialogo con Antonio Negri sull'abitare nella metropoli contemporanea'. Posted on 16 July 2015 on EuroNomade at http://www.euronomade.info/?p=5228

15. Reflections on 'Manifesto for an Accelerationist Politics'

Translation of 'Riflessioni sul *Manifesto per una Politica Accelerazionista*'. Posted on 11 February 2014 on EuroNomade at http://www.euronomade.info/?p=1684

Chapter 16. Notes on the Abstract Strike

Translation of a speech at the *AbStrike* Conference, S.A.L.E. Docks, Venice, 8 May 2015.

Chapter 17. From the Factory to the Metropolis . . . and Back Again

Written for the present volume.